*All*
*Manner*
*of People*

# All Manner of People

## THE HISTORY OF THE JUSTICES OF THE PEACE IN SCOTLAND

Johan Findlay

THE SALTIRE SOCIETY

All Manner of People published 2000 by
The Saltire Society
9 Fountain Close,
22 High Street,
Edinburgh EH1 1TF



A catalogue record for this book is available
from the British Library.

ISBN 0 85411 076 3

Cover Design by James Hutcheson

Printed and bound in Scotland by Bell & Bain Limited

## *Contents*

This book is dedicated to the memory of

***JOHN MAXWELL OF BROOMHOLM***

Justice of the Peace 1764-1799

An Exemplary Justice

# *Preface*

Shortly after being appointed as a justice of the peace curiosity as to the origins and history of the office led me to the surprising discovery that there was no single volume on the subject. A brief history does appear in older manuals for justices but to someone with a deep interest in history this was only enough to encourage the search for more.

The book, *Scottish County Government in the Eighteenth and Nineteenth Centuries* by Ann E Whetstone was an invaluable aid in beginning the research as was Sir Thomas Skyrme's *History of the Justices of the Peace.* Recent academic research by Dr Elizabeth K Carmichael and Dr Lionel K J Glassey has been very helpful and I am grateful to them both for permission to use material from their theses.

Over the four centuries of their existence in Scotland, justices of the peace have given a great deal of time and energy to create a court that is efficient and effective despite much opposition from the legal profession. There is certainly a feeling, to paraphrase Nigel Walker, that if criminal law is the Cinderella of jurisprudence then the summary court presided over by lay justices of the peace must be Cinderella's illegitimate baby! The baby has come of age.

Though the power and influence of the justice courts has waxed and waned over four centuries they have are always returned, refreshed and ready, to take up new challenges of extended jurisdiction. There are great advantages in any system which encourages lay people. In a democratic society where rule is 'by the people' a much greater awareness of the system is created by the participation of lay members while judgement by one's peers creates a sense of legitimacy and justice. James VI was perhaps ahead of his time in introducing justices of the peace to Scotland – a king whose mother was beheaded may have less than altruistic motives for limiting the powers of hereditary barons – but the office of justice has certainly contributed to the maintenance of social order in Scotland since his time.

The *raison d'etre* for the justice system is that a local person with understanding and knowledge deals with local transgressions. As well as describing what justices could, and can do, under the law, I have tried to include as many examples as possible of the justice in action, dealing with real cases. These were 'real'people who for some reason or other had broken one of the rules laid down by society being tried by justices of the peace who were also 'real' people. Many of these justices worked diligently with an increasing workload over the years to maintain the Commission of the Peace and have fought to improve the office for the benefit of all concerned and it is because of this that I have dedicated this book to the memory of John Maxwell J.P. of Broomholm who was one of the many. We are today what our judicial forebears created, just as our work will help create the future for those justices who follow.

Many people have helped and encouraged me with this research and I am indebted to them all. In particular to Sheriff Principal Gordon Nicholson QC, Sheriff Peter G B McNeill QC, Sheriff Lewis Cameron, and Sir Thomas Skyrme KCVO, who so willingly and with unfailing generosity gave advice and pointed out the right paths to follow. Douglas Beck and Desmond Park require special thanks for help and guidance and I would also like to thank Thomas C Smith J.P. for permission to use his letter. Both Ian Fraser and Jane Richardson, the past and present Secretary of Commissions, answered my many questions both promptly and courteously and the staff at the Ewart Library in Dumfries, particularly the infinitely patient Geoff Creamer, were most helpful. The same is true of the staff at the Dumfries Archive Centre, especially Marion Stewart, and at the National Library of Scotland, the University of Edinburgh Library, Register House and the Public Records Office in London. The Saltire Society have been very helpful in the preparation of the publication and my thanks are due to the Society's editor, Thorbjørn Campbell, for his invaluable advice and guidance.

I am indebted to those friends Phyllis, Alastair, Eilidh, Andrew, Ron and others who encouraged and supported me along the way. It is not possible to mention everyone by name but my thanks go to all who have helped in any way – this must include Ralph who saved the manuscript from electronic meltdown! To my family, David, Stephen, Louisa, Raymond, and Siobhan a very big thank you. Finally to a special friend, Kitty, thank you for being there.

While acknowledging the help received from so many colleagues and friends, I must of course emphasise that all errors or omissions are mine alone!

J.F
Lochmaben
October 1999

# *Introduction*

Justices of the peace, who voluntarily sit in the district courts of Scotland today, are bound by their judicial oath which holds the grave promise 'to do right to all manner of people after the laws and usages of the realm, without fear or favour, affection or ill will.' It has been stated by J. Irvine Smith that justices 'have never played more than a minor part in the administration of our criminal law. It should be said, however, that the evidence for the other side of the story is still largely inaccessible. Perhaps when it becomes available in print it will be necessary to amend the traditionally accepted account of the role played by the justices in the 17th century.' It is hoped that this account will go some way to redress that situation and present the other side of the story of the justices of the peace from the earliest days to the present.

There is no doubt that the justices were, in the main, conscientious but often faced difficulties and frustrations for which they received very little help or guidance. Lay justice, which is simply the judgement of one citizen by another, is as old as the history of man and certainly much older than any formal legal system. As long as two or more people have lived together there has been the need to have rules for the benefit of the community as well as the individual and when the rules were broken – as broken they must have been – there had to be some way of dealing with the transgressor.

Down through the centuries an increasing number of rules and regulations have been introduced by courts and by governments. Legal systems have evolved and lawyers trained to know and understand legislation with a complete judicial hierarchy created to sit in judgement. Throughout all this education and enlightenment the system whereby lay people judge the facts in criminal cases has been retained. Juries, justices and judges decide issues of fact in a court of law, not as professionals, but as fellow citizens.

In 1975 with the District Courts (Scotland) Act, the office of justice of the peace was revitalised when the burgh, police and J.P. courts were amalgamated into the district court and the jurisdiction increased. The J.P. today has only two duties; to sign certain papers and documents and to sit as a judge in the district court. Both of these functions reach as far back as the foundation of the office but the original work of the justice of the peace extended far beyond this jurisdiction. In the past many other unpaid and frequently quite onerous services were performed for the government.

The office of justice of the peace has existed in England for some 700 years and in Scotland for almost 400 years. Throughout this time the principle has remained the same, that lay people who are living and working in the community have the experience, local knowledge, and understanding necessary to deal with those who contravene national or local law. The status of the Commission of the Peace has fluctuated through the centuries from being almost totally eradicated to becoming an essential component of the criminal justice system, and has matured from being the pawn of political patronage to becoming a player with complete judicial independence. Justices are appointed 'on behalf and in the name of Her Majesty by instrument under the hand of the Secretary of State and a justice so appointed shall only be removed from office in like manner.'[2]

Today the position of justice of the peace is conferred upon all manner of people in stark contrast to previous years when only wealthy landowners and noblemen were considered for the office and 'judgement by one's peers' was unheard of for the commoner. To fully understand the present day institution of the Commission of the Peace and the men and women who serve on the bench as justices it is necessary to appreciate the compelling history which lies behind this ancient office.

## References

1. J Irvine Smith in *An Introduction to Scottish Legal History* (Edinburgh 1958), p41.
2. District Courts (Scotland) Act (1975), c20, p9.

CHAPTER 1

# The English Experience

After an abortive attempt in 1587[1], the Commission of the Peace was finally instituted in Scotland in 1609 because of the overwhelming success of the English justices, whose office had already been in existence for some three centuries and whose history can be traced far back to medieval England.

As early as 1195, amid great unrest during the reign of Richard I, when the establishing of some sort of law and order was high on the list of priorities of the monarch, a medieval 'vigilante' force was put into operation. This group comprised males over the age of 14 who swore to obey the laws and never become thieves or vagabonds and would pursue any criminals when ordered. The knights who took the oaths of this group were given powers to try suspects who were held in prison. Following this the *custodes pacis,* the conservators or keepers of the peace, were established with duties to 'arrest all malefactors and keep them in safe custody while awaiting orders from the Crown.'[2]

During this era there was great unrest and social tension, with constant threats of riot and rebellion. The king realized that keeping law and order on a national scale had to start locally on a formal basis without giving too much power to these local officers. Against this background of escalating crime these keepers of the peace were established. It is noteworthy that Scotland was suffering from similar problems when the Commission of the Peace was established there in 1609.

In England by 1361 the need had grown for a more formal approach and a statute of that year provided 'For the better keeping and maintenance of the peace [the king wills] that in every county good men and lawful, which will be no maintainers or barrators in the county, shall be assigned to keep the peace.'[3]

## *THE FIRST JUSTICES*

1361 has always been considered the date of the inception of the justices of the peace as that was the date of the statute which first uses the title 'justice of the peace'. However, as has been seen, their origins are much older and created through need for a local administrative and judicial process accountable to the king and independent of the lords. One of their duties was to ensure that the sheriffs in England were efficient. The duties and functions of the English sheriffs were gradually usurped by the justices.

The transition from keepers to justices of the peace was not an entirely smooth passage. Many rules and customs were created within communities that were not on statute books and the men designated to be these new justices of the peace were the local landowners or knights who knew and understood both the local rules and the people living there. They also knew the laws of the kingdom and as local landowners were men who were most likely to be respected and held in some awe by the community. Not least they were men who had a vested interest in maintaining harmony in the surrounding countryside:

> a fundamental characteristic of the justices ... was that they were local men with their own independent interests firmly established in the areas in which they were required to function, and with a personal concern in the lives of the other inhabitants of the neighbourhood.[4]

Their powers as keepers of the peace were fairly limited and consisted mainly in arresting suspects and enquiring into other crimes but not to try those accused nor to deal with those found guilty. This lack of authority caused much criticism and there were heated debates in Parliament with one faction stressing the importance of local knowledge and others wanting a special commission comprising lawyers and magnates. However the House of Commons won the debate and in 1361 the statute which created the title of justice of the peace also gave them the powers to determine their own cases thereby achieving a more satisfactory situation. Indeed Charles Beard comments:

> The justices were chosen from the most stable elements of the gentry, scattered as permanent residents through every county. They possessed that intimate knowledge of local persons and conditions which facilitates efficient administration but they never secured enough corporate independence to endanger the cohesion of the national system. No continental state possessed such a combination of local independence

and central control and England's early national unity and internal administrative uniformity were in a large measure due to the institution of the Justice of the Peace. [5]

### *ORIGINAL AUTHORITY*

Gradually justices of the peace received authority to deal with economic and administrative matters as well as their criminal jurisdiction. This development was particularly important when the Black Death was rife in England and Europe as it became apparent that consequent economic difficulties led to unrest and violence. The Black Death did not present the same problem in Scotland as communications were poor and travelling extremely difficult. Communities in Scotland were remote and so cross-infection was not as great a risk as in the insanitary, overcrowded towns of England where the loss of over one third of the population to the disease was disastrous. The drop in the numbers of agricultural labourers gave them a strong bargaining position with the landowners who attempted to impose a massive wage freeze. Added to this, the end of the Hundred Years War with France left soldiers demobilized and unemployed with perhaps little choice but to exercise the ability to pillage learned in war. The newly appointed justice of the peace had to begin his work under these very difficult circumstances; but there was none better to act than a respected local figure of authority with an acquired understanding of his community. However, he had no jurisdiction over men of greater rank than himself, since the Privy Council handled cases involving such people.

### *THE ENGLISH SHERIFF*

The English sheriff was not a supporter of the justice of the peace since the creation of this office undermined his position as the most important official in the shire. The sheriff was the governor of the county with responsibilities for collecting the king's taxes as well as having judicial authority, but his duties gradually diminished in importance. An Act of 1461 assured the justices of supremacy when all indictments normally reserved for the sheriff were to be taken before the justice of the peace. Medieval England had a variety of courts and all were expected to take action in serving the community, but as the same officials sat in many of the different courts it was not important which court dealt with each matter.

### *THE 1361 ACT AND THE APPOINTMENT OF JUSTICES*

The Act of 1361 was particularly clear concerning appointments of justices:

> In every county in England there shall be assigned for keeping the peace, one lord and with him three or four of the most respected in the county, with some learned in the law and they shall have powers to restrain the offenders, rioters and other barrators and to pursue, arrest, take and chastise them according to trespass and offence.[6]

It is assumed that the fact that the trial was not mentioned was inadvertant, since it was made clear later in the Act that the justices were to 'hear and determine the felonies'.

Only peers of the realm and landowners, many of them lawyers, were appointed as justices and by 1439 they had to have an income of at least £20 per year. This monetary qualification remained until 1906 by which time the amount had risen to £100. In the early days the English justices were paid for their services at 4 shillings per day for a maximum of 12 days in the year, but peers of the realm were not paid and, in an effort to economize on public expenditure in later years, there were simply more peers appointed.

### *SUMPTUARY LAWS*

There was never a shortage of laws over the centuries for the courts to deal with although many must have been virtually impossible to administer or even to detect. Sumptuary laws describing in great detail what men could wear or not and which material the garment should be made up in were designed to preserve class distinctions or occasionally to support the linen or wool trade. Dogs could not be owned by people of less than a certain income, football and tennis were forbidden to the lower orders and there was even a law forbidding anyone to wear a nightcap sporting a silk tassel![7]

Justices of the peace were expected to take a moral stance to prevent their fellow countrymen from the evils of excessive adornment in dress or over -indulgence in any pastime which could possibly endanger the immortal soul. Somerset justices tried to have the alcohol content of ale reduced in case the youth should become corrupted and begin a life of sin, depravity and gambling.

### *SENTENCES IN ENGLAND*

Sentencing determinable by the justices in England at that time comprised fines, flogging, banishment from one county to the next, branding, mutilation and eventually, from 1586, transportation. Prisons were used only to hold the accused until the trial or until their debts or fines were paid. During this period there were debates on whether the fines should be determined by the ability of the convicted to pay or purely by the nature of the crime. In Scotland at least the Acts of Parliament stated that the offender was to be fined according to his means.

### *ADMINISTRATIVE DUTIES*

Justices had many very onerous administrative duties which again were unpaid and which in fact were very probably subsidised out of their own wealth. These duties included the raising of capital required for major road and bridge construction projects and overseeing their execution plus their ongoing maintenance. Each landowner in the county was obliged to aid the justices by providing men and equipment for 6 days' work in filling pot-holes, clearing out ditches, and any other appropriate work.

Increasing traffic on the roads necessitated these chores being carried out frequently and lack of scientific knowledge of road-building meant it was very basic and temporary. Local farmers ploughed up roads, obstructed the way or even altered the course to suit their farming policies, all to the extreme inconvenience of road users. Roadways were the only internal lines of communications and it was of vital importance to keep them open particularly as trade began to flourish. Tolls on bridges which dated back to medieval days now became the province of the justice of the peace, the money used to help pay for the upkeep of the roads and bridges.

Under Tudor monarchs the justices were given jurisdiction in fixing the price of grain for the area. This was an important job with widespread ramifications as the price of grain decided the price of bread and so it was incumbent on the justices to prevent speculation in times of famine and poor harvests. During these years of crisis they were expected to search granaries and barns to determine what quantity of grain was stored and justices were empowered to ensure farmers brought specific amounts of grain to the weekly market.

### *POOR LAW*

The poor were a perennial problem and once again this was laid at the justices' door. Feeding and caring for the poor was in fact one of the major preoccupations of the justice of the peace during the 16th to 18th centuries. The poor, basically the lower orders of society, could number two-thirds of the population. Underprivileged commoners covered the spectrum from small shopkeepers and tradesmen to labourers, paupers, thieves and vagabonds. Not all those people were destitute but extreme poverty was a threat which hung over them permanently. One bad harvest and they were faced with unemployment and starvation. When this happened, to survive they had either to become criminals or to receive support from the county. It was of course advantageous to the justices as local landowners and landlords to help the poor and destitute because the next stage was riot and rebellion. How much easier for all concerned if the problem could be contained! Unfortunately the success of the Poor Law was totally dependent on the local administration within each shire or county and there was a considerable amount of carelessness on the part of some of the justices at a time when the office was very onerous. The poor created an even bigger burden at times of famine or a particular crisis within any of the trades, and this in itself would directly affect the justices.

### *BOOK OF ORDERS*

In 1630 the English government produced the *Book of Orders* for the justices which was an attempt to instill new vigour into the flagging magistracy and inspire their enthusiasm to sustain the burden of administration. It allowed the Privy Council to examine and enquire into the work of the justice and revitalized the Poor Law as well as organizing all the laws created over the previous 30 years. The one 'Book' covered amongst other things, basic farming, apprenticeships, and the regulation of ale-houses.

The *Book of Orders* set out the whole package very clearly so that even the most unlearned of justices were quite aware of their duties both locally and to the government. It was of primary importance during the civil war when parliament rarely sat. The justices themselves sat infrequently at quarter sessions throughout this period but local administration had to continue. Justices who saw membership of the Commission as a stepping-stone to becoming members of parliament and those who were already members met often and kept open the debates.

Under Cromwell the justices of the peace had their powers extended, since the Lord Protector appreciated the effectiveness of the rule of local administrators. Inevitably many of those loyal to the Crown were removed from the commission and their places given to those whose sympathies lay with parliament. The civil war in England had thrown the courts into turmoil as the counties took sides. Cromwell replaced local gentry with men of lesser calibre and even less social standing with the inevitable result that these had little respect among local people. Cromwell gave the justices powers over those who were greater in rank than themselves, something which had always been expressly forbidden: previously men of rank who committed crimes had to be reported to the privy council and dealt with by those lords. The withdrawal of men who had been brought up with the very necessary paternalistic attitude to their countrymen, left the office in the hands of men unequal to the vast administrative chores and whose lack of authority was frighteningly obvious in these years of uncertainty. It was only with the support of the militia that the authority of many justices was maintained.

The legal expertise of the English Bench was safeguarded by rules that a certain number on the bench had to be 'of the quorum', that is, learned in the law as the original statute ordered. However the bench seldom included anyone who was legally trained. The clerk of the peace, was in fact required by statute to be in court to assist the justices to deal with necessary paperwork, but it was not until the Justices' Clerk Act 1877 that the clerk had to be a solicitor and was paid a salary instead of fees in England.

### *THE QUORUM*

The original meaning of the word quorum, 'of whom', came from the Act appointing the justices **of whom** (it stated) that **some** should be learned in the law. Courts could not be held without including this 'of whom', this selected **quorum**. 'By the eighteenth century ... the 'quorum' was rendered meaningless by entering all justices as members of it whether or not they had any legal knowledge.'[8] The Latin word gradually came to mean in English the number of justices required to constitute a court. This number changed over the centuries but two or three were needed for most proceedings and their jurisdiction was substantially reduced with fewer justices. Successive acts of parliament actually stated the number of justices necessary. Even today a single justice in England is fairly rare and he has very limited powers. In Scotland, by contrast, justices sit singly or in threes with no difference in their powers. The quorum was abolished by an act of 1753.

Justices held their quarter sessions in the courts in the town and as many magistrates would turn up as felt like it – the more interesting the case or administrative duty the more justices would attend. Smaller sessions, called petty sessions, could be called any time and would often take place in the local inn or the justice's front parlour with just one or two attending.

Those justices of the peace who were not of the quorum had several books to guide them in their work. Lambarde's *Eirenarcha*[9] of 1581 remained in use for over a century. The 600 pages describe very fully the responsibilities and duties of the justice of the peace. Printed pamphlets were circulated when specific problems required more detailed information. The justices were reminded at all times that they were under the supervision and control of the privy council who ensured their orders were carried out.

The House of Commons did not approve of the right of the Privy Council to question the work of the justices. This impasse meant that the Privy Council had only one method of exerting its authority, namely dismissal from the Commission. This was used as a political or religious manoeuvre and did not add to the prestige of the commission of the peace

The rights of the individual or the accused were protected, theoretically at least, against the amateur or even downright biased ways of local magistrates – always assuming they were articulate enough to complain. However central government went to great lengths to ensure that the justices were able to carry out their tasks not only effectively but within the framework of the law.

### *QUARTER SESSIONS*

The quarter sessions, so called because they met quarterly, were the local administrative and judicial meetings where the justices sitting with juries made up of local worthies, decided such issues as maintenance of the roads and bridges, administering the poor laws, licensing alehouses and hearing criminal cases. Over the centuries the justices were given progressively more administrative work as the population grew and expansion of industry created more traffic on the roads. Courts dealt with such crimes as witchcraft, poaching, drunken brawls, theft and numerous other incidents although it was considered that only a small number of crimes were actually taken to court; the majority were left unreported.

One of the thankless tasks of the justice of the peace was to appoint a constable for the area. The job was unpopular and grossly underpaid as the constable was considered to be on a par with the gamekeeper – a man who betrayed his neighbours. Yet another burden placed on the justice's already laden shoulders was that of the lieutenancy and militia. The Lord Lieutenant rose to power in England during the 16th century as a local military official who appropriated the military jurisdiction of the sheriff at this time, thus partly eroding shrieval powers. His function was to organize and train the local militia who were to defend the crown against foes or invaders. Often the Lord Lieutenant appointed a deputy who would in fact bear the brunt of the work; he was usually a local landowner and commonly a justice of the peace and his task entailed gathering together the fit men of the county and training them into some semblance of a military force. He was responsible for keeping lists of all the equipment, uniforms, armour and weapons and ensuring that there was an adequate supply of bullets and gunpowder and that the warning beacons kept at strategic points were ready to be lit in the event of an invasion. Duties involved collecting money or even organizing supplies of grain for the market in times of trouble.

However despite brief flurries of activity and a vast number of regulations from the government, the militia in England never really achieved a position of much importance. There was neither enough enthusiasm nor enough money to maintain armaments. The justices were empowered to call out the militia in times of violent unrest – assuming they were close enough and ready and able to come out. There were occasions when the justice lived too far from the rousing point for effective action to be taken in time.

Many noblemen retained their own private armies whose services were offered to the king when required. This practice was also common in Scotland. Here the militia did not come into being until the 18th century after the fear of arming a potentially hostile population had receded. The government relied instead on the aid of Scottish nobles and their retainers for military support in emergencies, sometimes issuing them with specific warrants granting them the title and powers of the English Lords Lieutenant.

As administration in England gradually became more cohesive, combining all the separate units, the bulk of this administrative work was firmly vested in the justices of the peace who maintained a balance of power acceptable to central and local authorities.

Throughout the 18th century more wealth was created by industry than by landowners. The *nouveau riche* had arrived. A new social sphere took shape as society adapted – albeit grudgingly – to accommodate the mutual dependency of inherited wealth and industry. Suddenly the property qualification of the justice of the peace opened the office to the industrial barons and a new era began in the history of the commission of the peace

### *CORRUPTION AND THE BASKET JUSTICES*

In England towards the end of the 18th century, particularly London and Middlesex, the office of justice of the peace went through probably the most shameful period of its history. Corruption was rife in every walk of life and there was a massive crimewave – theft, murder, and arson. Justice was a commodity available to the highest bidder: the 'Basket Justices' of the 17th century who openly received goods in baskets as gifts was still there in the 18th century. Hugh Walpole wrote, 'The greatest criminals in the town are the officers of justice. There is no tyranny they do not exercise, no villainy in which they do not partake.'

There were a few notable exceptions in the persons of Thomas de Veil and John and Henry Fielding who despite taking payment for their services were regarded as scrupulously fair and honest in their dealings. Henry Fielding had the distinction of being the first publicly-paid stipendiary magistrate. Others had been paid out of secret service funds.[10] He was a notable playwright and lawyer as well as the author of *Tom Jones.* He played an important part in the history of the theatre and it was due to his satirical attacks on the government that the Licensing Act of 1737 (which survived until 1978) was rushed through parliament, making the Lord Chamberlain the licenser of theatres and requiring that every new play should be sent to him to be read and approved prior to performance. This was instrumental in bringing about the censorship of plays and, paradoxically as a justice of the peace, Fielding had a duty to enforce this law. However as a justice he was particularly effective and active in the suppression of ruffianism and thuggery in the streets of London.

Severe game laws were brought in and enforced with a vengeance by the landowner justice who in this new era, safeguarded property above everything else. Poaching by the father of a starving family could result in transportation for 10 years. The poor law was never more required than in the decades around 1800. However these game laws and the zeal with which they were pursued were probably the significant factor in the fairly rapid decline in prestige of the justice of the peace in England. Such justice represented a harsh legal system which was totally contrary to needs of the starving and unemployed who saw the workhouse beckoning. Children well enough to work were apprenticed to employers who in many instances were simply uncaring slave-drivers. Since the justice of the peace had legal, administrative and economic charges he appeared omnipotent and inescapable, and when the desperate starving poor threatened rebellion he could call out the militia.

By the early 19th century the use of juries at quarter sessions for administrative work such as the repair of roads and bridges, was reduced to mere formality and a process of more direct administration gradually evolved with paid officials supervising the structure of roads. Justices were ordered to hold their courts only in authorised places so sessions were no longer held in the front parlour or the local hostelry. Courts began to distinguish between judicial and administrative work and finally with the formation of the police force the justice ceased to be both judge and detective as the police took over the task of prevention and detection of crime.

## *LEGAL REPRESENTATION*

It was not until 1836, and amid great opposition, that a lawyer was permitted to represent the accused in the magistrates' court in England; indeed it was considered that it could be damaging to the accused to have a lawyer speak for him. In 1831 a lawyer was forcibly ejected after arriving at Cheltenham court to defend his client. The Chief Justice of the day ruled that justices had complete discretion in allowing lawyers to appear before them and considered that justice would be served 'without that nicety of discussion or subtlety of argument' for lawyers. In 1796 Patrick Colquhoun wrote, 'No sooner does a magistrate commit a criminal than recourse is made to some disreputable attorney, whose mind is made up and prepared to practise every trick and device such as getting depraved persons to swear an alibi that can defeat the ends of justice.'[11] This contrasted with the situation in Scotland where the lawyers upheld the tradition that no-one should be tried without a defence agent.[12] This dated from an Act of 1672 which entitled the defence to the final speech in all cases other than rebellion or treason. History always records the extremes and the history of justices of the peace is no exception.

There were many instances of severe treatment of offenders but there are many more stories of the great paternal element whereby people were shown leniency and understanding. Justices of the peace have, throughout their existence, been close to their own communities and, as Sir Thomas Skyrme points out in his *History of the Justice of the Peace*, 'service on the Commission of the Peace made the justices more aware of the shortcomings of the existing system and of the misery which these caused.'[13] There were as many contemporary writers who were supporters of the justice of the peace as there were critics.

### *PRISON REFORM*

It was widely believed that only extreme harshness of sentencing would quell the crimewave swamping the large cities but eventually humanitarian ideas began to emerge and a gradual awareness of the need for social reform created improvements in housing, workplaces, prisons, and actual disposals from court. At one time prisoners were kept in appalling conditions with total lack of sanitation and hygiene.There was no segregation of prisoners either with regard to their sex or to the nature of the offence.

The rapid growth of humanitarian reform and social welfare in Victoria's reign saw the emergence of government officials who gradually undertook the administrative work of the justice. Factories, mills, and mines were established with huge workforces and these were to be inspected by Crown Agents – the Inspectorate of Workplaces. Inspectors of prisons took over from the justices their role in the maintenance of jails and surveyors were appointed to oversee the roads. The poor and needy became the responsibility of the parish commission. A vast number of authorities was set up to deal with these urgent problems without much co-ordination, so that at first a confusing bureaucratic network resulted. This however was shortlived and the appearance in 1888 of the county councils was a great relief. Many of the administrative burdens, which could never have been foreseen at the inauguration of the justice of the peace in 1361, were transferred to elected councils and although many councillors were still justices the duties were now shared with others. The justices retained their judicial powers and those of the licensing board.

Justices continued to be chosen from the landed gentry as indeed were the first elected councillors but over the years the new social strata created by the growth of industrial wealth brought changes and manufacturers, mill owners and bankers came to the fore. The Commission of the Peace also found itself drawing on a broader spectrum in the appointment of justices and the modern trend of selecting from a cross-section of the population began.

In 1910, following a Royal Commission, the Lord Chancellor brought in the first Advisory Committee to put forward nominations for appointment, the property qualification having been abolished in 1906. It was not however until after the First World War in 1919 that a true cross-section of the public was eligible to be justices when women were allowed to sit on the bench. The English Magistrates Association was founded a year after this but training did not become compulsory in England until 1966 – six hundred years after the establishment of the justice of the peace. Today in England the justices deal with some 97% of criminal cases, including all traffic offences except causing death by dangerous driving.

Borough courts in England were the town equivalents of the county's justice courts and were in existence alongside the justices' office. These courts were amalgamated when the county councils were formed. The magistrates who sat on the borough bench were the mayor with two or three of his aldermen – it never grew to the size of the county bench. It was not quite as democratic as at first appears, since only certain members of the community had a vote. They were not considered to be of the standing of the county justices who tended to feel superior and who would not allow tradesmen on the county bench. The only judicial strike in history was over the possible appointment of a grocer in Wales in 1833.[14]

The jurisdiction of the borough magistrate was much less than that of his colleagues on the county bench and he dealt with no more than minor assaults and misdemeanours. The bench was small and self-perpetuating being confined to members of the corporation who were tradesmen or craftsmen of the town. Sadly, the borough bench often did not have the ingrained local awareness and connections which had proved invaluable down through the history of the justices. Borough magistrates were further confined by a fairly limited period of office making the sustaining of any particular policy quite difficult. Overall they contrasted strikingly with the county bench who were remarkably free of the corruption so rife on the borough bench. The siuation was so bad, particularly in London, that stipendiary magistrates were substituted. Stipendiaries were introduced in other parts of the country as well after some years.

For six centuries lay justice in England survived and developed under the influence of continuous social and political change. The control mechanism it offered central authority, whether King or Parliament, came to be highly valued and it was no surprise when it was introduced north of the border after 1603 when the Scottish and English crowns were united in the person of James VI and I.

## References

1 APS 1587 c57 vol iii p459b.
2 Frank Milton, *The English Magistracy* (London 1967), p3.
3 1361 34 Edw 3 c1.
4 Thomas Skyrme, *History of the Justices of the Peace* Vol. (Chichester 1991).
5 Charles A Beard *The Office of Justice of the Peace in England* (New York 1904), p71.
6 1361 34 Edw 3 cl.
7 Milton, *op. cit*, p9.
8 E Burney, *JP Magistrate, Court and Community* (London 1979).
9 William Lambarde, *Eirenarcha* (London 1581).
10 Milton, *op. cit.*
11 Patrick Colquhoun *A Treatise on the Police ofthe Metropolis*
12 (London 1796), quoted by Milton, *op. cit*, p49.
APS 1424 c24 vol ii p24.
13 Skyrme, *op. cit*, xi, p131.
14 Milton, *op. cit*, p14.

CHAPTER 2

# *The Scottish Justice of the Peace*

It was against the background of the tremendous history and wealth of English experience that James VI instituted the office of justice of the peace in Scotland in 1609.[1] He had lived with the Scottish problems of wild and unruly Lords, and watched minor squabbles grow steadily more serious. James was also heavily influenced by Elizabeth I and impressed by the more civilised appearance of England where the very efficient and cheap Commission of the Peace was established. He decided a similar arrangement would work equally well in Scotland.

Prior to this an attempt to introduce an office bearing the title the 'King's Justice' was made in 1587 along with an attempt to re-introduce circuit courts called Justice Ayres. These were to be held by eight judges appointed by the king from among the Senators of the College of Justice or from experienced advocates who would travel round the kingdom adjudicating in the name of the king. The justices on the other hand were local men who were to help organise the ayres and arrange for accused persons to be brought to the justice ayre when it came to the area. Appointments were made for every county in Scotland and the appointees were to be 'honourable and worthy persons, in degree earls, barons, knights and special landed gentlemen experimented in the lovable laws and customs of the Realme and living in the shires.' They were granted 'full power to take inquisition and make dittay by their own knowledge and by sworn inquest or sworn particular men, of all persones suspected culpable of the crimes and defaultes conteined in the Table.'[2]

All serious crimes were to go before the circuit court, with lesser crimes to be dealt with by the king's justices at their own courts to be held four times a year. Dates for the justice ayres were set up all over Scotland, starting in Linlithgow on 27th November 1587, covering all the main towns and ending in Orkney on 21st February 1588, a hectic schedule by any standards. The plague however, hit Edinburgh and all courts were cancelled for two or three months. On 29th December 1587 James announced his regret that the Justices Ayres had been put off 'through God's visitation of the pestilence' and he 'discharged and annulled all commissions of lieutenancy and justiciary granted by His Highness and ordered them to have no further effect in time coming.' The king's justices were abolished before they had the chance to serve. The justice ayres did not achieve success until 1672 when the High Court of Justiciary was established. [In 1797 an appeal to the Lords Ordinary brought about the comment: 'a complaint for shooting pigeons founded on the acts 1567 and 1597 c.20 cannot be competently brought before justices of the peace (they) have no jurisdiction under the Scots statutes passed long before their appointment.'][3]

James finally introduced the Commission of the Peace in 1609 to 'extirpate the ungodlie barbourous and brutall custome of deadlie feads.'[4] The Scots, a century behind their southern neighbours, were not enamoured of the imposition of 'foreign' principles and remained highly suspicious of the new justices. The general feeling was that the country had done very well before the justices and there was no need for them now. Much of the hostility came from heritable jurisdictions where handsome profits could be made in their courts. Administratively the concern was well founded as Scotland, unlike England, did not have the squirearchy to support the justices.

## *MEDIEVAL SCOTLAND*

Prior to the 13th century the legal systems in both Scotland and England had developed along similar lines under Roman and Norman influences but the all too frequent wars between the two countries including, of course, the Wars of Independence, created a schism forcing them to go their separate ways. England developed her own independent legal system very quickly and had little need for outside involvement while Scotland remained under continental influence, notably that of France, Italy and the Netherlands. Scottish students desiring to further their education went abroad to find tutors on the continent. There they learned the art of debate and advocacy and the skills necessary for a lawyer, with many of them returning to teach their fellow countrymen in the Scottish universities. Even as late as the 16th century advocates studied in France, then renowned as the home of legal study.[5] England exerted no influence on Scots law until, after the Union, when there were vain attempts to amalgamate the two kingdoms' systems. The English common law on which the justices prided themselves was quite different from common law in Scotland and this was to prove problematic at the inception of the Commission of the Peace.

***THE COURTS***

Medieval courts in Scotland were numerous - baron courts; guild courts; head courts; and even forest courts as some of the forests belonged to the King. They were both administrative and judicial in function in a country entrenched within a feudal system where servitude was not questioned but freely given in return for patronage and protection. Servitude included the right of the lord to demand that his men give military service for him when necessary and protection of the vassals and servants meant that justice would be meted out for them by the lords in these separate courts.

The baron, sheriff, lord or noble who presided over these courts was theoretically under the authority of the king. These judges had limited jurisdiction in that the four pleas of the Crown, namely murder, rape, arson and robbery, were reserved for the king to deal with personally but other crimes and offences – breaches of the peace, theft or assaults – were all dealt with at local courts. The king kept control by making these judges accountable so that, in theory at least, anyone remaining unsatisfied could appeal to the Crown in the hope of receiving justice. The theory was excellent but was probably not put into practice very often: sadly, few records remain. Many of these courts were heritable jurisdictions, guarded jealously by the nobles and were to prove to be a thorn in the side of the justices when they were eventually established. Few, if any, of those dispensing justice in these courts had any training in the law and legal procedures.

The burghs were first created around 1120 and they flourished over the next few centuries. These burghs were invested with valuable rights to trade and with the holding of regular fairs and markets to the detriment of those towns not designated 'burghs.' Burghs also had monopolies in the manufacture of certain goods such as beer or bread. They were much needed at the time as a method of stimulating the economy but the same restrictive practices were eventually to exert a negative effect on the nation's economic growth. The burgh became powerful and self-perpetuating whereby the old burgh council chose the new.

Local government was of the greatest importance to the inhabitants of each burgh and certainly of much more immediate concern than national government in medieval Scotland.At the October 1535 head court at Selkirk an inquest of 14 men under the alderman and bailies appointed 'ane inquest of the best and worthyest unsuspekit men to decreit and to decerne rycht and wrang for a year to come.'[6] These 29 men were ordered not to be absent without good reason when called by the bailies or be fined 12 pennies. The inquest varied in size and there does not appear to have been a statutory number. As noted previously, Scotland lacked the squirearchy or manorial system that gave the justices of the peace their strong position and authority in England. The Scottish parliament was not influenced by commoners. Justices in England were often the same men who sat in parliament and they were made aware of public opinion when they met at quarter sessions. The practice in Scotland was that only the great lords and important clergymen attended parliament. Thus there was a limited role for public opinion.

### *THE SCOTTISH SHERIFF*

The office or role of sheriff had existed in Scotland since the time of King David I in the 12th century and the influence of the office holders could be found throughout Scotland. The office embraced duties with regard to both criminal and civil law, but like his English counterpart, he also had to collect the royal revenue or taxes. This was the familiar role of the English sheriff of folklore. In Scotland the sheriff was usually the local noble who had great judicial powers. Prior to the 16th century judgement was by the whole court, the assembly of suitors, with the sheriff acting as president giving direction on points of law and procedure. Juries were empanelled for both civil and criminal cases.[7] Later in the century the sheriff became the judge and juries were used only for criminal actions and very limited civil work. The sheriffs appointed deputes to perform their duties and they in turn appointed substitutes, none of whom was obliged to have had any legal training although it is probable that most did.

The shortcomings of the sheriff substitutes were a constant source of complaint and this led to numerous counteracting acts of parliament. James VI appointed a commission to study any illegal or wrong decisions by the sheriffs but it does not appear to have met. After the justices of the peace were appointed it was stipulated that the justices were to check on the conduct of the sheriffs and report any who defaulted in their duties. This was, not surprisingly, an unsuccessful measure and was reversed eventually; the justices were supervised instead. Some two thirds of the sheriffs held an hereditary office and succeeding monarchs attempted to abolish hereditary sheriffship but in all cases it proved to be not only expensive but offensive to the great nobles.

The power of the hereditary sheriff was shown in 1582 when Thomas Cuming of Altir complained about the Sheriff of Elgin and his friends, two of whom were sheriff deputes. Cuming had obtained a decree from the lords of council and session in March 1582 granting him exemption from the jurisdiction of this sheriff. Notwithstanding the decree which had been published in the usual fashion at the market crosses of both Elgin and Forres, the sheriff along with several friends had laid siege to Cuming's house carrying off a servant and putting him in the 'pitt in the most vile conditions'. The servant was later tried, wrongfully convicted as a thief and then executed, despite the decree of exemption being shown in the court. The sheriff and his deputes were denounced as rebels but their names remained on the lists and it is probable that nothing was in fact done. While this account may not be typical of the times it does nevertheless show an example of the power held by the sheriff.

The sheriffs suffered the same fate as the justices during Cromwell's time: they were replaced by men loyal to the régime. These men, who sat with an army officer, were applauded for their impartiality and efficiency.

The jurisdiction of the hereditary sheriffdom was preserved in the Act of Union. However, following the 1745 Jacobite Rising, the Heritable Jurisdictions (Scotland) Act 1746 finally abolished the hereditary judges and provided that the office should be by crown appointment. Prior to 1748 the title or style 'sheriff' or sometimes 'sheriff principal', had been an hereditary title for the lord or indeed lady[8], of the county who usually delegated the powers to a legally qualified depute to perform the work involved. Often he in turn would, as already noted, appoint a sheriff substitute who did not require to be legally qualified, although in practice those so appointed may well have been practising solicitors or advocates. The abolition of the hereditary title in 1748 meant that a legally qualified judge was appointed to the post, retaining the title of sheriff depute. The act also gave the deputes power to appoint sheriff substitutes in areas where it was deemed necessary. The Sheriff Courts Act of 1825 required that all sheriffs must have been qualified in law for at least three years. In 1828 the title 'depute' was removed and it was not until 1971 when the 'sheriff' (depute of old) was styled the 'sheriff principal' and the 'sheriff substitute' became simply 'sheriff'. The office of sheriff grew in power as the workload increased and gradually overtook the role of the justice of the peace.

### *JUSTICIARS*

Justice emanated from the king. He would travel over his kingdom to promote it as a socially stabilizing influence, but it was hardly feasible for him to cover the length and breadth of the country within a reasonable period of time. In the 14th century two justiciars were appointed, for 'north and south of the Forth' and later more were appointed to supervise Galloway and Lothian. These men went on 'ayres' or circuits twice a year through Scotland and were to keep open communications between the monarch and the local communities. This was important to establish the supremacy of the king as the fount or promoter of justice and the final authority in appeals when local justice failed. This office was quite inadequate to the needs of the people, particularly as courts were only held irregularly in times of trouble. Further statutes throughout the following centuries attempted to revitalise the office which in 1672 was destined to become the now well-established High Court of Justiciary

The justiciar went on ayre or circuit to hear cases with further responsibilities in overseeing the work and administration of the thirty or so sheriffs in Scotland. As well as taking action on those who evaded their duties, he had a ministerial function in measuring land in the many boundary disputes when the area was walked around or perambulated and the marches agreed. The justiciar also had the duty of maintaining the peace and was able to call out soldiers to put down any minor rebellions. Acts for keeping the general peace in Scotland were passed as early as 1449. Justiciars sat at the king's parliament to witness papers or documents and to take part in any local and papal courts. They could hear cases involving the Four Pleas of the Crown, sitting as the king's depute.

Scottish history is peppered with attempts by the monarch to break the power of the magnates and lords in private and public courts. Creating the Circuit Court was one of the attempts which was successful and has remained. The number of attempts is indicative of just how much power these lords yielded and the difficulties pertaining to them. James VI wrote in his *Basilikon Doron* (a book of advice to his son) that the heritable sheriffdoms were 'the greatest hindrance to the execution of our laws.'

Rules and laws of medieval Scotland were very detailed and recorded along with judicial procedure. Sentencing would almost certainly include compensation for injury to the victim or kin and a fine payable to the king. Compensation was meted out strictly in accordance with the class or rank of the injured party. The compensation took the form of cows or pennies to avert a blood feud. 'Striking without blood was valued at 10 pennies.' David Walker states in his *Legal History of Scotland* 'these rules were probably an idealized statement and not necessarily workable but the basis was there.' Compensation continued after 1587 when the crown took over the bulk of prosecution of crime and it was possible to escape the gallows by a pecuniary award to the victim. Indeed a prosecution could be prevented by paying the crown and the victim. This practice did not die out until the 18th century when the Lord Advocate instituted most prosecutions.

Over the centuries the office of justiciar waned and the ayres became less frequent until they virtually died out altogether. By 1514 the position of Lord Justice General had been created and a permanent criminal court set up in Edinburgh in 1524. Attempts to re-establish justiciars were made in 1587 in an Act which stated that two justices depute appointed for each quarter of Scotland would hold justice ayres twice a year . Lesser crimes would be heard by men similar to English justices of the peace who would be appointed in each shire. Neither of these ideas, however, came to fruition.

The Act of 1587[9] names each sheriffdom or county and states the number of 'worthie persons being knawen of honest fame and esteemed nae meintainers of evill or oppression,' to be appointed as the king's commissioners and justices. They were specifically to be men who lived in the area. Each shire was to have a certain number of these men – 7, 14 or 21 – depending on the size of the shire, and along with four men from the burgh council. However the plague intervened and the establishment of the 'justices' James VI had visualised remained a paper enactment, local justice was dispensed as always before by the local lords or sheriffs in their heritable jurisdictions, or by a depute appointed by the lord justice general for their area. Scotland was suffering from yet another period of economic confusion and hardship fuelled by depreciation of the coinage by parliament. In such a climate it is not surprising that any expensive innovations remained only as intent.

Bread and ale had always been the most important commodities and in 1496 an Act ordered provosts and bailies to examine the quality and price of bread and ale. Maintaining a plentiful supply at reasonable prices to the populace was vitally important to prevent social disorder. By statute the price and weight of bread was controlled by the burgh authorities. These 16th century problems continued into the 17th century, bread and ale still remaining as important commodities. The reign of James VI in Scotland was marked by a permanent shortage of money since the coinage was constantly being devalued. This in turn caused sharp rises in the price of food and an equally sharp drop in the standard of living. Bad harvests and famine which affected the whole of Europe caused further economic distress with a critical rise in the price of grain and subsequently of bread. The pricing of bread was the province of the English justice of the peace and James VI's social control policy was deeply influenced by the English experience.

During the last two decades of the 16th century, Scotland underwent further unrest, arising from the tensions provoked by religious controversy and the perennial problems with the nobles. When James accepted the English crown he was further impressed by the peace-keeping abilities of the English justices. He had shared with Elizabeth a horror of war and deeply desired to have peace in his kingdom. Besides, the English justice appeared to be equally effective in dealing with famine, vagrancy and witchcraft, the last a personal obsession with James.

Lack of finance for radical social control policy was one of the biggest single problems facing James, so the willing unpaid justice of the peace was trumpeted as the obvious answer. But Scotland aleady possessed an elaborate and complicated court system which left virtually no room for the justice, unlike England where he had been enshrined for 300 years and was totally incorporated within the legal system and social order.

James VI had an uneasy relationship with the church. State and Kirk each wanted to control the other or at least to be able to wield a good deal of power in each others' province. James wanted the ministers of religion kept to their business in the Church, and an Act forbidding them from any judicial position was passed in 1584. The Act stated:

> that the ministers of Godis word and sacraments may the better and mair diligentlie attend upon thair awin chargeis and vocatioun, Thairfoir statutis and ordainis that all the saidis ministeris sall lawfullie await thairupon to the comfort and edificatioun of the flokis committit unto thame and that nane of them presentlie being in that functioun or that sall be admittit theirto in tyme cuming sall in any wayis accept, use or administrat any place of Judicature in quhatsumevir civil or criminall cause, not to be the College of Justice commissioneris, advocatis, court clerks or notaris in

> any matters (the making of testamentis onlie exceptit ) under the paine of deprivatioun from thair benefices levings and functioun.[10]

This Act must have been taken seriously because it remained uncommon to have Scottish ministers on the Commission of the Peace and in some parts of Scotland even as late as 1837, it was considered to be illegal to appoint ministers.[11]

### *INNOVATIONS TO THE SCOTTISH LEGAL SYSTEM*

Although the office of lay magistrate had not been established in 1587, James VI had success with several other innovations in the Scottish legal system including reform of the High Court, improvements in criminal court procedure and the introduction of the Lord Advocate as public prosecutor.

It was possible for the litigants or witnesses to approach the jury when it was enclosed or during an adjournment. This practice was disallowed by forbidding adjournments from day to day and by ensuring that all evidence was put to the jury in the presence of the accused. This had the effect of dealing expeditiously with trials but was taxing on the jury who had to sit continuously until the case was finished, no matter how long. The accused was to be allowed the services of a lawyer, unlike the practice in England where defence lawyers before 1836 were expressly forbidden to speak for a client in court.

### *LORD ADVOCATE*

The Lord Advocate had always been the Crown representative in civil cases but the Act of 1587 gave him the power to prosecute all crimes even in instances where the victims or their families did not consent, and he was legally protected from any retaliation from the accused or his family. This alongside several restrictions on private prosecutions in Scotland meant that nearly all prosecutions for serious crimes were brought by the Lord Advocate or his deputes. The Lord Advocate's representatives, the procurators fiscal, were originally the collectors of fines in the sheriff courts (Collection of fines required proof that a crime had been committed.) Their powers were extended when the workload of the sheriff courts increased after the abolition of heritable jurisdictions. From earliest times each court appointed and paid its own fiscal until 1907 when the appointment was vested in the Lord Advocate.

### *INSTITUTION OF THE COMMISSION OF THE PEACE: 1609*

James VI needed local officials, loyal to the crown, who would attempt to keep the peace, stop any unrest from getting out of hand and who would be responsible for reporting to the crown any of the heritable jurisdictions not fulfilling their obligations to justice. The Act of 1609 gave the crown the right to appoint justices of the peace in each shire on an annual basis. Oddly enough the same omission was made with this Act as was made in the original English act concerning the emergence of the keeper of the peace in 1195. Although they were to catch, take and present suspects for trial they had no powers to try these suspects themselves: this left the justices disheartened and with very little sense of satisfaction despite extensive efforts on their part. The situation was rectified two years later when they were given jurisdiction to try suspects and impose any punishment thought necessary.

### *KING'S GUARD*

Prior to 1603 there was no local agent to enforce the enactments of the Privy Council other than the barons and lords who did virtually as they pleased, including setting up juries to give the verdict required. In 1603 a body of mounted police was instituted to execute decreets of the privy council and to apprehend criminals. This group, called the king's guard, was to cover the central part of Scotland but it was disbanded fairly suddenly in 1611. 'The reason given in the warrant for this unexpected act was that His Majesty found "no grite use or necessitie" for the maintenance of so expensive a body.'[12] The main reason was that a much cheaper county administrative body had just been created – the justice of the peace.

### *THE ACT OF 1609*

The Act of 1609[13] lay dormant for a year when the Chancellor, the Earl of Dunfermline and the Earl of Aberdeen were commanded by royal letter to appoint justices of the peace but even then lists were not ready until October,[14] and not made public until November 1610.[15] The royal letter stated that those appointed were to be "suche personis whom in both your judgmentis you do understand best affected in religioun, fordward in our service and lovers of our peace, and frie of all wrongeing or oppressing of thair nichtbouris in tyme past." The letter goes on to say "and to gif unto thame such instruction is to be keipit and observed in the executioun of thair chairge as you sail hold fitting and expedient."[16]

Further to this the Lords of Council granted Thomas Finlayson, a printer, the monopoly to print Acts of Parliament and articles concerning the justices of the peace and the constables. Thomas Finlayson was to hold this privilege for 20 years; all other printers were discharged from printing any of these and booksellers were prevented from selling any Acts of Parliament printed by any one other than Finlayson. [17]

The justices were expected to take some responsibility for understanding their work. English justices had many books such as Lambarde's *Eirenarcha* (1592), Dalton's *Country Justice* (1618) and Bohun's *The Justice of the peace, His Calling and Qualification* (1693). Training books for justices were not a new idea and, as the office in Scotland was based on the English experience, Scottish justices were able to make use of the same material.

The Act of 1609 was fairly short and simply laid down the foundations for the Commission of the Peace. The preamble however gives us a very good description of life at the time:

> foolish words or drunken discords between subjects of greatest rank and their meanest servants and dependants and any other in the country did so readily embrace the protection of their unjust and unnecessary quarrels as did many times involve themselves and their whole friendship in most bloody and mortall troubles which they did prosecute with such malice and cruelty as to the extreme peril of their souls.[18]

It continues: 'considering that nothing gave so great growth and strength to that bypast barbarity as the sloth of magistrates on not suppressing the first seeds of these dissensions which were small and weak in the beginning ... these light jarrs and insolences were then easily to be settled if diligence and authority were to be joined'. (The 'magistrates' mentioned above are any judges or town bailies.) The Act stated justices were to be appointed yearly with their main remit to be the prevention of crime. They had power to

> command all persons in whom they shall see manifest intention to make trouble or disorder by gathering together of idle or disorderly persons or by publicly bearing or wearing of pistols or other forbidden weapons and such other riotous and swaggering behaviour, to bind themselves and find caution under competent pains to observe His Majesty's Peace.

At first the justices had no powers to deal with the offenders themselves but had to present them to the lords of privy council or his majesty's justice. However by an act of council in 1611 the justices were given authority to try those offenders who were below a certain status and a further act of council in 1612 declared

> in the tryall of the contraventioun of penall statutes whairof the paine is pecuniall not corporall and the tryall not appointed be the laws of this realme to be ane assize then the justices of peace sall proceid in thair tryall be confession of party, aith of veritie, or witnessis.[19]

In other words any case not involving a jury and not carrying corporal punishment could be dealt with by the justices.

### *PROCEDURE DURING THE 17th CENTURY*

Taking the oath of parties in court was normal procedure: they were assumed to be telling the truth if they would take the oath. This practice continued for some time. In the oldest justice of the peace sederunt book available, that of Peebles,[20] dated 1659, one entry states that two people had been brought to court for committing ryot (i.e. assault) and 'there being no otherways able to prove the same refer it to the defenders' oath who sworn depone negative and are absolved.' The oath was taken personally in court.

James VI was determined that the justices should be successful and every encouragement was given to them. As a way of stimulating those appointed to carry out their duties, he announced that it was no small honour to be appointed a justice of the peace. The main frustration was the continued influence of heritable jurisdictions. But those disobeying the justices were answerable to the Privy Council and there are many instances of the powers of the council being brought to bear on those who offended. A group of men in Kirkwall in Orkney in 1612 who assaulted a man with a sword leaving him for dead, disobeyed an order of the local justices 'to enter into ward'. The matter was referred to the Privy Council and despite the accused not appearing, the lords found the charges proven including disobeying the justices. They were ordered to be held in the tolbooth in Edinburgh within 40 days under pain of rebellion.

A similar case is recorded at Perth in 1612 when Patrick Blair refused to remove the guns and pistols he wore, contrary to the Act of 1611 prohibiting the same. Although the justices had spoken to him privately he still refused and was ordered to come to court but made no appearance on the day. Being summoned anew to a further sitting which was to take place in the Kirk of Lundlief with 4 justices, the quorum required then between quarter sessions, he arrived at the court but threw down the citation, having struck the table with his fist and behaved contemptuously even to grasping his sword, but was put out of the kirk before he could use it. In the kirk yard he assembled 20 or 30 of his friends and threatened the justices. Blair was ordered to appear before the lords of council where he admitted his guilt and was warded in Edinburgh tolbooth at his own expense and at his majesty's pleasure[21].

There was much opposition to the justices by the burgh magistrates and in 1612 the justices of Linlithgow complained that the magistrates would not give the oath to the bench to allow them to take their place. The justices of Selkirk wrote to the lords of council in 1611[22] stating the problems they had with the magistrates of the town. They went on to say what they felt should be done about the beggars. The letter shows great understanding about local needs and problems plus the difficulties faced by the poor of the parish. It reads:

> We have according to your Lordships commissioun undertake and begin our charge by appointing of constables and chusing stentouris and collectouris of the taxatione for the puir and sall be most willing to do quhat farder our travellis may effectuant the furtherance of his Majestys service in that office. Whairin our greatest and only impediment is the towne of Selkirk thair obstinat refusal to concurre. Who being conscious of thair owin disorderis whairoff this haill countrie compleins, and not knowing how to cloake and keip them from the just tryall of our censure otherwyse nor by ane fals protest off thair owin privilegis they would neither accept nor acknowledge our commissioun; so that we are the more doubtful to do any guid service in the office till your Lordships give ordour thairanent. As concerning the ordour appointit to your Lordships for suppressing of the sturdie and idle beggars and supporting off the trewlie puir and indigent, we both allow of it and sall gladlie follow it in so far as the present estate of this puir shireffdome will permit; which being for the most part of his Heiness propertie and consisting haillilie off store rowmes and subtenantis, who notwithstanding that their yeiris bygone the wairis having neither passage abroad nor giving any

> pryce at hame, has been the subject to the yeirlie payment off deiw maillies, few duties and continuall taxationes whairwith they be so exhausted and impoverished that they be scarselie abell to interteine themselffs far less able to help otheris; and albeit they would condescend to the maintenance of the trewlie indigent and impotent within their owin shireffdome yit the great number both off the sturdie who will not work and the off othereis who are willing bot can have none, will be still ane great burdeine to the land, there being no jayellis to hold the one or imploy the other. It were wishit that your Lordships would appoint some commoun work in everie paroche, as the mending of hieways or suchlyke, whereby the idill may be forcit, the willing imployit, bothe interteined and the countrie disburdeined And for to gif lyff and beginning to this motion wald it pleis your Lordships to assigne the fynes of these ryotts quilke sail fall within the compass of our tryall to be imployit in such sort as your Lordships sail prescryve, we think that his Majesties peace would be better mainteined and the puir peipill the better interteined.

A select committee was detailed to discuss the problems between the burgh magistrates and the justices in 1612. The result was that the magistrates were to meet with the justices at quarter sessions and have the same powers and privileges held prior to the justice's appointments. Any acts or ordinances made by the justices were to be implemented by the magistrates. It was also decided that the payment to the justice's clerk should be 40 pounds per year, payable out of the fines.

### *THE OATH*

The original oath taken by the justices in 1610 bears a great similarity to the one taken today, stressing the need for impartiality and fairness.

> Ye sall swear that as justices of peice in the cuntrie of ... all artickles in the Kingis commissioun to you directed, ye sall do equall rycht to the pure and to the ritche after your cunnyng, wit and power and after the lawes and customs of this realme and statutes thairof maid, and ye sail nocht be of counsell with any persone in any quarrell hanging befoir yow and that yow hold your sessiounes after the forme of statutes thairof maid and the yssues, fines and amerciaments which sall happin to be maid and all forfatouris which sall fall befoir yow ye sall treulie caus to

be entred without any concealmant or imbesealing and treulie send thame to the Kingis exchekquer. Ye sall not let for guifte or uther caus, bot weill and treulie ye sail do your office of justice of the peace in that behaiff and that you tak nothing for your office of justice of the peace to be done, bot of the King and fees accustomed and costs lymited by the statute and ye sail nocht direct or caus be directit any verrant by yow to be maid to the pairties but ye sall direct thame to the bailies of the said cuntrie or other the Kingis officeres and ministeres or other indifferent persones to do execution of thairof. So help you God and by the contents of this buik.

As today, this oath was followed by the Oath of Allegiance.[23]

### *APPOINTMENTS TO THE COMMISSION*

Lists of justices were made up on a yearly basis but they were not always accurate or kept up to date. On the 24th July, 1612 Lord Sanquhar was reappointed to the Commission of the Peace despite having been hanged some weeks previously on the 29th June of the same year. The story involving him is indicative of the brutality and power of the nobles and the lack of impartiality in the judicial court unless under duress. Lord Sanquhar was a man who enjoyed great notoriety arising from his prowess at fencing. He agreed to a contest with a fencing master called John Turner, who, during the match, put out one of Sanquhar's eyes. Some few years later Sanquhar was a guest in the court of the King of France who learning the history of the loss of the eye inquired, 'Is he still alive, the man who did that?'

Sadly Sanquhar was determined on revenge and on his return to England promptly hired a Robert Carlyle who shot Turner with a pistol. Sanquhar absconded but returned when he learned that £1000 had been offered for his head. He admitted the murder and threw himself on the Kings' mercy

There was a great deal of anti-Scottish feeling in London at this time, the chief cause being the insolent behaviour of the young Scottish Lords in the royal court. King James VI, who had left Scotland for London in 1603, had little option but to consent to the execution of the sentence and Lord Sanquhar was hanged outside the gates of Westminster on 29th June 1612. James was unable even to save him from the commoner's death by hanging as opposed to decapitation: 'for the grater contempt of our nobilite he was hangit among a number of thieves' but his execution did appease the vehemence of antipathy to the Scots.[24] Robert Crichton, Lord Sanquhar, had been appointed a justice for Perth in 1610. His son, William was appointed after his father's death in July 1612.

Many justices were uneasy because the rules under which they had to carry out their duties were not clear enough. One of the main causes of complaint was that they were in constant danger of losing business to other courts since they were forbidden to deal with a case until 15 days had elapsed from the time of the justices' citation. This meant that often nothing was done until it was too late. In March of 1612 a group of justices asked the Privy Council a number of questions, one on the subject of the 15 day rule. The Council refused to change the rule to the evident dismay of the justices:

> this interim 15 days frustrated and made void their service and simply made them just serjeants and officers to the other judges in the country while they with the hazard of their lives has at the first committing of any wrang or appearance of commotion and trouble, taken pains and travel in their own persons (as they ever do to stay all further trouble) to assure His Majesty's peace and arrest the offenders to their answer, then the other judges will take upon themselves the tryall and decision of that offence and way which by the justices has been settled and pacified and the fines taken by the other lords, prelate or baron as they (the justices ) do not get the fines personally but only have the peace of the country and public good in the aims.[25]

The rule was obviously an attempt to keep favour with the holders of the heritable jurisdiction but paradoxically the justices were also given jurisdiction to oversee the work of sheriffs and bailies and report any who were remiss to the Privy Council.

### *THE ACT OF 1617*

Corruption was widespread in the administration of justice during the 16th and 17th centuries with few courts free of royal or political influence.[26] Bribing of judges or court officials and the intimidating of witnesses and juries was common. In 1579 an Act stated that lords of session nor their wives nor servants should take bribes.[27] In comparison, the later Cromwellian courts appear to have been models of impartiality and fairness which was so unusual that it was commented upon.

In 1617 James VI appointed a committee of four to appraise the sum required to compensate for the total eradication of the heritable jurisdictions which were notoriously corrupt. The committee were also to revise and amend any sentences thought to be inadequate which had been imposed by the sheriffs and they were to report any instances of the sheriff failing to act. The ever-present financial difficulties of the Scottish Parliament prevented the abolition of the heritable jurisdictions but some of the sheriffs were made to surrender their offices with renewal possible on a yearly basis if they could pay the king's dues. This left the holders of the heritable courts, namely the Scottish aristocracy, with vast judicial control and ability to oppose effectively any alternative legal system.

A massive Act of Parliament in 1617 set down in great detail the duties of the justice of the peace and those of the constables they were to appoint to help them. The Act included the oath to be taken by the justices, by which they swore to do equal right to rich and poor, to conform to the laws and customs of the land, to decline jurisdiction if they had any personal interest in any matter before them and to keep the quarter sessions and more when required. The oath of nearly 400 years ago has stood the test of time and is echoed in the judicial oath taken by the justices of today.

### *THE QUORUM IN SCOTLAND*

While the English quorum distinguished between those justices who were 'learned in the law' and those who were not, the distinction does not appear to have existed in Scotland. The quorum simply meant the number of justices required to hold a legally constituted court.[28] The Privy Council had decided in 1612 that four should be a quorum but under the Act of 1617, however, the quorum was to be three justices deciding matters outside of the quarter sessions, but a single justice had jurisdiction to bind any suspects to keep the peace whether reported to him personally by the victim or by an account from a constable. The justices had no jurisdiction over people above a certain rank, nor over prelates, counsellors and senators of the college of justice: these were to be dealt with by the privy council. Anyone refusing to appear before the justices was to be served with a warrant signed by any one justice and delivered to the accused by a constable

The Privy Council, as supreme judges of the kingdom, were to be informed by the jusices of any case which the sheriff or bailie court had not acted with sufficient severity. The justices were empowered under the 1617

Act to make some sort of recompense to victims. However the justices had no power to deal with the offender should the bailies or sheriff be specially lenient with the accused. They could simply report it to the lords of council. The 1617 Act states after every mention of a fine that it should be 'according to the qualitie of the crime and the estate of the offender'. This remains a requirement under statute for both justice and sheriff in today's courts. Compensation to the victim or his relatives was common then and like a fine was meted out strictly in accordance with the status of the victim.

### *THE DUTIES OF THE JUSTICES*

The Act empowered justices to act against a wide range of activities considered prejudicial to good order in society. They were, for example, ordained to use all their powers to restrain the lords and nobles from starting riots and rebellions as there was a great fear that a simple breach of the peace could escalate into a major event with one faction taking arms against another. Great emphasis was put on preventive justice by ordering the accused to find caution to keep the peace. 'Vagabonds, unemployed, anyone lurking in alehouses' and 'Egyptians' (gypsies) were all singled out for the attention of the justice of the peace, as well as those who housed or otherwise encouraged their idleness. People who 'slept all day and walked about at night' were considered highly suspicious. 'Nightwalking' appears to have been a problem in Scotland for several centuries. In 1540 Edinburgh, Peebles and Selkirk all shared the same rule that no one was allowed out after 'bedtime' other than on lawful business. Crimes occuring after dark incurred much higher penalties and would be dealt with by a higher court than the burgh. The term 'vagabond' included the following descriptions of people:

> jugglers, users of crafty or unlawful plays, [that is, unlicensed] sorcerers, gypsies, counterfeit idiots, and pretended deaf and dumb persons, fortune tellers, and others professing to have knowledge in charms, and the like, besides minstrels, songsters, and tale-tellers, not being in the service of the lords of parliament, or the great burghs. And to this must be added the ordinary paupers who beg even within their own parishes.[29]

This gives an idea of the numbers being dealt with and the suspicion which was immediately attached to anything at all out of the ordinary or to those who appeared to have 'unnatural' powers one of which was acting.

It was by the Act of 1617 that the justices were first invested with administrative duties. It authorized them to make and maintain all highways and roads to market towns or sea ports as well as the main road to the parish kirk. As trade became more important it was necessary to maintain the roads and keep lines of communication open. These repairs were to be done 'with the least grief to the subjects'. Anyone spoiling the roads or blocking ditches was to be punished. Roads were to be made at least 20 feet broad but any roads already made and of greater width were to retain their present size.

Offenders to be dealt with included destroyers of orchards and young trees, stealers of bees and beehives, breakers of dove-cotes and rabbit warrens, gamblers, poachers or anyone found with poaching equipment, forestallers at the market, hostlers giving hospitality to known convicts, rebels and beggars. The hostlers were to be dealt with by the baron on whose land the incident occurred but if the baron chose not to proceed then the justice was to have jurisdiction. Owners of illicit stills were to be sent before the king's treasurer or advocate for punishment and finally, justices were empowered to organize 'a state of emergency' in case of plague descending upon the country and to punish severely anyone not complying with these rules.

Plague, which could decimate the population, created severe problems and drastic measures were taken to prevent its spread. In Edinburgh in 1530, a woman who concealed her sickness was sentenced to be taken to be drowned and a man who crossed Edinburgh to go to St. Giles while his wife was ill with the plague was charged with 'affecting' the whole town and sentenced to be hanged on a gibbet outside his own door. However the rope broke and 'at the will of God' he escaped. As he was 'a poor man with small bairns' it was decided to simply banish him from the town of Edinburgh for the rest of his life. There is no record of what happened to his wife or children, but it is interesting that the sympathy extended to him came after the hanging attempt – he was after all 'a poor man with small bairns' prior to the sentence! The ale houses were to be closed at 10 o'clock during the course of the disease as a method of reducing infection.

Quarter sessions in February and August were to decide the wages paid to labourers, workers and servants. Those not paying the fixed rate were to be imprisoned and punished. To ensure that the servants would be more willing to accept the fees, the justices also enforced punctual payment of the agreed sum. Wages for a servant at that time could include '3 quarts of wool and a pair of shoes', or '9 pounds of wool and forty shillings Scots.' Justices were to ensure that there were adequate prisons and that they were kept in a state of repair. They were also to maintain any prisoners who were without the means to feed themselves while they were detained awaiting trial, having been committed between sessions. The parishes helped to raise this money.

The justices were to check that sufficient single and double ale was brewed in each shire but to fine anyone over-indulging in the same. Historically burgh magistrates had been responsible for ensuring that enough bread and ale of good quality were produced to feed the local inhabitants and this rule was an extension of that duty.

The burgh magistrates were expected to implement all directives in the towns. Drunkenness does not appear to have been recorded as a crime in Edinburgh until the early 17th century. Bread and ale had always been the most important commodities in the country and both were required to be of good quality. Each brewing of ale was priced by the justices. This had previously been done by the burgh magistrates who tasted the ale and fixed the price according to the cost of malt. Bread was priced in much the same way and in accordance with statute. A study of the burgh records of Selkirk in 1540 explains the procedure;

> A firlot of wheat was sent to the common mill to be ground into flour which was then baked into bread, being watched all this time by the bailies. This bread was known as the 'pais' or standard loaf and other loaves were to be judged by it. Bakers who sold underweight bread lost their livelihoods. All bakers were then given a standard loaf and if they broke the 'pais' by selling underweight bread the bailies were empowered to confiscate the bread and break the ovens of the bakers concerned.

Pricing each brewing of ale happened in much the same way, by the burgh 'aletasters or Connars, who took an oath to taste the ale and lawfully to apprise the same according to the price of malt.'[30] Bread making was governed by many rules for several centuries, with size, quality, price and composition all coming under the scrutiny of justices. With trade improving it was imperative that the weights and measures throughout Scotland be standardised:

> because there is sensible prejudice seen and felt through many parts of the kingdom by reason of the great diversity of measures and weights used in the same therefore our Sovereign Lord with advice aforesaid for removing of all abuses which may ensue in any time to come.

The standard was to be the 'Measure of Linlithgow', although it was to be a great deal later before a genuine 'national standard' was in use. A committee of 12 men all named in the Act was set up to decide how these measures should become the legal national standard for Scotland. The ruling, when made, was to be conveyed to the justices for implementation in each shire, the burgh magistrates dealing with the towns.

***PAYMENT TO JUSTICES***

Justices were to be paid expenses of 40 shillings Scots per day up to three days at each quarter sessions but lords, bishops and earls were not eligible for this payment. However any justice not attending the sessions without a reasonable excuse and who was receiving the allowance was to be fined 40 Scottish pounds. This payment was comparable to that made to the English justices who received 8 English shillings per day for up to 12 days in the year. Any extra-sessional duties could be claimed through the sheriff.

At the end of the quarter session a minute of the proceedings was to be sent to the Privy Council who could comment on the report if they desired and deal with any matter at the next session. This minute was written by the clerk of the court who retained a record of the proceedings. A *custos rotulorum* was to be appointed, by the king, from the justices and invested with special powers, one of them being the right to appoint the clerk of the court. This office was of English origin and died out very quickly in Scotland.

While it was always preferred that the clerk should have legal training it was not made compulsory until 1975. The 1937 manual for justices by J. Campbell Irons states, 'It is not necessary, but it is highly expedient that he [the Clerk of the Peace] and other deputes, be qualified lawyers of standing and experience.' In practice most clerks were in fact qualified lawyers

The justices were to appoint constables in each parish to assist them in arresting suspects, serving warrants, transporting persons to jail and pursuing any escapees.[31] It was an under-paid unpopular job and its popularity was not increased by the fact that constables were to be given part of the fine imposed when they libelled an accused. Some justices did not conform to this injunction quickly enough and the following August brought a subsequent act of council requiring those who had not done so to comply immediately.

The king was determined that justice should be seen to emanate from the Crown and not be dispensed on the whim of local lords, so law and the king, had to be available to every person from peasantry to nobility. Whether or not the peasantry were articulate enough to complain is debatable; James VI wrote in his *Basilikon Doron* in 1599, that the Scottish nobles had a 'feckless arrogant conceit of their greatness and power' and advised his son Henry, for whom the book was written, to visit all his kingdoms at least every three years 'hearing your selfe their complaintes.'

Several more acts of parliament increased the powers of the justices, but despite this the prestige of the Scottish justice never reached the height of his English counterpart, mainly because their position was not effectively defined within the intricate network of courts north of the border. Their lack of prestige in Scotland was also in part due to the national characteristics of a people not easily impressed by title. Scotland did not possess the squirearchy of England nor did it pretend to understand or emulate that social hierarchy. (This was to change, however, by the nineteenth century: much to the detriment of the Commission of the Peace, the honour of being a justice was more important than performing the duties.)

### *NUMBERS OF JUSTICES*

The number of justices on the original Commission of the Peace was about 420 but the working total was considerably less since many landowners were named for several shires. For example, the Archbishops of St. Andrews and Glasgow are mentioned 15 and 11 times respectively. It would appear that there were comparatively few justices in Scotland who were active.This number rose through the years, again with the first few names repeated, and those on the Commission were considered the cream of Scottish society.

The heritable jurisdictions continued to be suspect and an item on the agenda of the Privy Council in 1612 read: 'What may the Justices of Peace perform for pacifying the country in case of the disobedience or negligence of the heritable officers or contempt of powerful men in the country'.[32] To encourage the justices and to ensure that the heritable jurisdictions were not allowed to interfere, the Privy Council decreed that the justices of the peace should be the only competent judges to deal with the particular acts set down for them; failing that the Privy Council themselves, or the Court of Session would deal with it. (Strangely enough, this became a problem much later when justices were strictly forbidden to deal with an offence if it had not been explicitly stated in the Act that their court was competent to deal with it. The result was that the justices became starved of work.).

### *TOUR OF SCOTLAND*

King James made his one and only tour of Scotland in 1617. Preparations for this took nearly a year.[33] The justices of the peace of each shire were to be responsible for the provision of horses and carts to be used, at the king's expense, when he was in their area. This caused a few problems since no one appeared to know exactly how many were required; one shire reported that there were simply no carts to be had. The people of Scotland were told to expect the king and a retinue of 5000 with an equal number of horses. Arrangements were made accordingly but in the event substantially fewer arrived so that the city of Edinburgh became overstocked with wine and further imports were banned.[34]

### *CHARLES I*

James VI died in 1625 with the main obstacle to the justices still *in situ*, namely the heritable jurisdictions. In the *Basilikon Doron* the king had written that 'the great hindrance to the execution of our laws is the great men in possession of heritable jurisdictions and regalities.' He had not been able to rid the country of them and his son did not fare much better. These courts had a system of 'repledging' whereby the lord could claim the accused as his vassal and either try him before his own court or simply afford him protection even from the state. It was little wonder that the lords did not readily relinquish such powers. Charles I requested the sheriffs to send lists of all the barons and freeholders to the Privy Council to enable them to appoint justices, appointments having terminated on the death of the monarch. The sheriffs were not quick to do this and were threatened with fining by the Privy Council if they failed to produce a list. The Act of 1617 was ratified in 1630 and again in 1633 and this would suggest that the Commission of the Peace was still not working as well as originally hoped. Since no records remain of quarter sessions held in this period it is difficult to assess the actual position.

Several Acts of Parliament were created during the reign of Charles giving the justices of the peace jurisdiction in certain matters. One from 1640[34] is 'an Act for taking order with the abuses committed on the Sunday by the confluence of people for hyring of shearers on Sunday'.

> Forasmeikle as the prophanatione of the Sonday is greatly occasioned in the tyme of hervest by the confluence of people to publick places as portis or streets of Tounes and Paroch churches of landwart everie Sonday from morneing to preaching tyme for hyreing sheireris the weeke followeing. Whereof also ther aryseth sundrie tumultis disorderis sueiring drinking and often feighting one the Sabboth day For remeed heirof the estaitis of Parliament presentlie convened by his Majesties speciall authoritie remitts the samene to be takine order with the Justices of Peace and kirke sessiones where the abuse shall be committed heirafter by the confluence of the said people and hyreing of the saidis sheireris upon the Sonday as said is As the saidis Justices and kirke sessiones shall find the saidis abuses then to be committed to deserve. [35]

The Act immediately following this stops the Monday market in several towns as 'the leiges are distracted from God's public worship on Sunday by having to travel to Monday markets on a Sunday.'

On many occasions in the early 17th century fees or allowances were not paid by the authorities. Sir Archibald Primrose, the clerk to the Privy Council and writer of the commissions of the justices of the peace, did not receive his fees between March 1640 and September 1641. At this point a Mr William Lumsden reappeared illegally from banishment and was ordered to pay the caution for this to Sir Archibald as his fee. Sir Archibald was not a poor man and there is no evidence that he suffered particularly during this time but he did wait an inordinate length of time for his wage.

There are several instances of fines being used to pay wages or fees to informers. In the Peebles records of 1656 a constable is paid out of the fine received, for informing the court about an accused.

### *OLIVER CROMWELL*

It was not until the time of the Protectorate that the office of justice of the peace in Scotland acquired significant power, when Oliver Cromwell established previously unknown levels of order and 'civilisation' on Scotland, in particular on the unruly Highlands. The English army which had overrun Scotland enabled four English judges to be placed on the national bench. Contemporary critics noted that they were renowned for their impartiality – no great commendation of the previous state of affairs.

The regime took over the administration and performed the tasks normally undertaken by the justices such as pricing grain and deciding on the quality of bread. Cromwell disbanded all courts, prohibiting all jurisdictions other than those authorized by the English parliament and brought in commissions to deal specifically with the administration of justice. Local unrest, however, remained, particularly in the Highlands, and it became apparent that unless this was attended to, more violence would ensue. As always the most effective way of dealing with local problems was with the local administration of justice by those who had a vested interest in a peaceable neighbourhood.

By ordinance Cromwell established a civil court called the Baron Court in Scotland in April of 1654 in place of the existing lords' courts. This was to be held every three weeks in 'every place which really is or hath commonly been known as a manor.' It was to be run on the same lines as a manor court in England and was to have jurisdiction over 'all contracts debts promises and trespasses whatsoever arising within the said manor, provided that the demand does not exceed the value of 40 shillings sterling, nor involve the freehold or title of the land.' This court sat with a jury.

General Monck who led the campaign in Scotland, wrote to General Lambert in 1654 suggesting that the re-introduction of justices of the peace would go far in maintaining peace.[36] This was agreed and in February 1656, Oliver Cromwell re-established the justice of the peace, having produced the *Instructions* outlining their jurisdiction in December 1655 in Edinburgh. The Commission of the Peace was an institution understood by the English and Cromwell had found that it was impossible to rule without it in England. The new regime naturally enough required men who would be loyal to the Protectorate and both justices and burgh magistrates were ordered to take the oath of fidelity to the Commonwealth before accepting the office, albeit with much protest. The rules or *Instructions* of the justices were published and displayed on the market cross of all towns so that 'all people of this nation ... may take notice and be observant of the said *Instructions* as the contravenors will answer at their perils and to the end that no person may pretend their ignorance of them.' The local inhabitants saw little difference, familiar as they were with a way of life where powerful men commanded respect. The men appointed to the new Commission of the Peace were men of some social standing and influence in the community with the necessary experience of local custom, but there were fewer of the aristocracy than before. To ensure the new judicial establishment remained faithful and adhered to the principles of administering justice, each commission area had a leading army officer appointed to serve alongside the local justices. The occupying army also helped bring suspects to court and kept down riots, thus conferring greater general authority on the justice. The military remained in control until after the Protector's death. Cromwell allowed certain of the Highland landowners to keep arms for the defence of those on their estates and made the clan chief responsible for the behaviour of his clan members. This worked extremely well and peace was maintained in the Highlands as never before. The boast was that a man could 'ride over Scotland with £100 in his pocket and a switch in his hand which he could not have done these 500 years.' Justices were required to issue passes to those people who wanted to travel in Scotland.

At this time trade was suffering badly and many Scotsmen lost their fortunes and estates through debts or forfeiture. Accordingly Cromwell ordered land and personal wealth to be assessed on a monthly basis and this taxation was retained after the Restoration as the cess tax. A Commission of the Assessment was set up with the announcement that the justices of the peace should also serve as commissioners of the assessment This was more important to the gentry than serving as a justice and, since there was a general reluctance to sit on the bench, an order was made to the effect that these men had to serve on both commissions or neither. Before appointment the officer in charge of each garrison had to find men willing to perform these tasks, loyal to the regime and living conveniently near to the court or session place.

Another duty which now fell to the justices was to counteract the 'great neglect in conviction of Popish recusants so that no penalties are levied which has induced many to imbrace Popery.' From 1655 an oath of 'denial of Papal supremacy, of transubstantiation, purgatory and image worship' had to be taken before any two justices of the peace, mayor or city officer who were to 'administer the oath as a necessary duty and not to do it or forbear at their pleasure.'[37]

Throughout the period of the Protectorate there were attempts to unify Scots and English law and the Scottish justices were given the same powers the English had enjoyed for three centuries. Quarter sessions were held regularly supported by the army. This removed any problems with the nobles as Cromwell gave the justices jurisdiction over all people regardless of rank. Binding over of suspects was important in nipping trouble in the bud. Kirk sessions lost their jurisdiction to the justices in an attempt to move ecclesiastical rule to the civilian court. Thus justices found themselves once more dealing with the morals of the community with powers to impose severe fines on any convicted of fornication, swearing or breaking the Sabbath. The clergy were so displeased at this loss of authority that the Scottish council decreed that half the fines should be used within the parish for the good of the community and the other half to be split between the constable and the informer.

The justice of the peace in Scotland at last had a foot on the ladder of the judicial hierarchy: it now had authority to bring before the circuit judges anyone suspected of serious crimes such as murder, treason, incest, or blasphemy, to oversee the work of the sheriff, to ensure he did not aid in the wrongful acquittal of criminals, and that he sentenced adequately. Administrative duties placed virtually the entire social and economic welfare of the community in the hands of the justice. They now had responsibilities for the sick and needy, and duties to supervise the contracts of labourers, to settle prices of grain and to keep communications open by maintenance of roads and bridges. The cost of all of this was high and had to be paid for out of taxation. In addition the upkeep of the military by a people who were already very poor was enormous.

In 1653, Cromwell abolished religious marriage services in England and replaced them with civil ceremonies performed by the justices. By 1657 there was so much protest that the ban on church marriages was removed although the power of justices to solemnize marriages remained until after the Restoration. Any marriages solemnized by them remained valid. It may be assumed that the position was similar in Scotland as there was a great move to have both countries under the same laws, and in the year between 1656 when the Scottish justice was re established and 1657 it is possible that Scottish justices had the power to perform marriages, although whether there was time for the new powers to be implemented is not known.

***INSTRUCTIONS***

The Cromwellian rules for the justices, to be repealed but imitated in the Recissory Act of 1661, were known as *Instructions* and were almost a copy of the 1617 Act. These *Instructions* came to be regarded as the principal legislation governing the duties of the J.P. well into the 19th century. Hutcheson states in 1815: 'the instructions of the statute 1661, c 38, which are little more than a fuller and more articulate statement of those of Oliver Cromwell in 1656 and King James's Act 1617, c 8, still constitute our only general code of laws in relation to these offices.'[38] These rules, with the weight of the army behind them, and the removal of the heritable jurisdictions opened the way for the justice of the peace to operate effectively. Far from destroying the rule of the nobility, it was moulded into co-operation with national law for the common good of the entire community and was on the whole accepted. Cromwell's justices were not drawn from the upper echelons of society as before, but were still men of some social status and the new system made great inroads into the stabilizing of Scottish social order.

By 1658 it was clear that the two legal systems north and south of the border could not be easily amalgamated and Scotland was given control over her own judicial system within limitations. Justices needed constant reminders of their duty to watch out for robbers with royalist sympathies. As in England two justices made a quorum.

A testimony to the effectiveness of the powers of administration held by the justices was shown during the interval between Cromwell's death and the return of the monarchy. There was no anarchy or chaos and the rule of the justices simply continued, despite the fact that circuit courts were not held for six months after the death of the Protector.

The oldest sederunt books for the justices of the peace are from Peebles and the book starts in 1656. The book is a fascinating insight into the daily lives of the local people as well as the work of the justices . The following comprises two day's entries in the book. The court appears to have sat on a weekly basis.

At Peebles the 23 May 1659.
Margaret Lachlan servant to James Noble in East Halpead complaining that the said James Noble would not satisfy her hyre to witt forty shillings scotts and nine pounds wool. The said James called compearing confesses

> the debt whereupon the Justices order him to pay the said Margaret Lachlan forty shillings money and the nine pounds wool or thirty three shillings six pennies for the same.

The hiring fairs were held three times a year and the girl had been hired but not paid. She would not be able to get other work before the next hiring fair and so would be left destitute. It is interesting to note the price of wool, and the fact that it was part of the hire. In later years it was common to include two pairs of shoes in the wage and farm labourers often received certain meals and foodstuffs such as potatoes.

> The constable in Eddleston delated [i.e. informed on] John Paterson and Margaret Laws for ryot they are ordered to be brought before the court the next day and witnesses prove the ryot. ['Ryot' was a very serious breach of the peace usually including assault.]

> Alexander Lauder and John Smart indwellers in Hucheonfield complain that John Dermott being feed to serve them refused to enter home according to the conditions The said John Dermott being called compeared and having nothing relevant to answer for himself the Justices ordain him to enter home to his service according to condition and for that effort to find caution.

The phrase 'to enter home' meant that the servant had taken up the post and indeed had entered the house.

> John Tweedie complaining on a servant woman who refused to serve him according to the Justices Acts the said John receive an order from the Justices bench to retain her or present her to the next justices of peace to be sent to Gaole. The justices adjourn their court to the 30 of May. Signed Jas Veitch.

The use of the word 'gaole' is most unusual in Scotland and it is possible, that as the date is 1659, there were English men in the court from Cromwell's regime as he put clerks (noted for their honesty) into the courts. The most common word was prison or simply 'tolbooth'.

At Peebles the 30 of May 1659. This day Commissioner Sir John Veitch and Mr John Hay of Haystoun Justices of peace. Sir John Veitch chosen praeses.

The Justices ordain the measures of Skirling deposit in James Horsburgh their officer hand to be broke inhibiting the inhabitants of Skirling or any others to make use of any other measures but these prescribed by the Act of Parliament to witt Linlithgow measures upon the pains contained in the Act of Parliament and such further punishment they shall think fit for willfull contument of the acts hereanent.

Much of the justices work over the centuries was in establishing a standard of weights and measures:

This day John Young paid in four pounds for Nicols fine for fornication committed in Skirling parish whereof he was paid back eighteen shillings for his service as constable. [A wonderful example of the practicalities of the local court when the constable is paid out of the fines there and then.]

John Matheson in Woodhouse having lain incarcerate for not paying fines imposed ever since the last day the Justices ordered his own band (i.e. bond) taken for his payment for said and James Stevenson in Haystoun cautioner.

Michael Halywell fornicator with Janet March compearing is fined for himself and the woman in nine pounds which he paid whereof the constable who libelled them got thirty six shillings . This fornication was in Lyn Parish. [Another example of paying the constable this time for information.]

The Justices adjourned the court to Monday the 6th of June 1659.

At Peebles the 13th of June 1659 [There is no reason noted for the further adjournment.]

This day Mr John Hay of Haystoun heard and discussed the bills following:

James Gillespie servant complained upon John Veitch in Lyne that he had served the said John Veitch he refused to pay him his fee John Veitch not being present is ordered to be summoned to answer the said complaint against the next Monday.

The only situation where a single justice could sit, was to order those involved to come to court. He certainly would not have been able to decide in any trials or make any decisions. Cromwell tried to recreate the powers of the English justices in Scotland and they never sat singly. The next entry in the sederunt book is as follows:

At Peebles the 26th day of December 1659. This day the Justices convened Sir Alex Murray Sir John Veitch Stanhope Sir Michael Naismith and Mr John Hay Chuse mr John Hay praeses.

The Justices having led and examined witnesses in Dawick and the Brouns bills finds them not sufficiently proven ordains the parties to have all the witnesses they intend to hear ready against the 9th of January continuing Brouns security And further they ordain both parties to give bond for keeping the peace which Dawick refuses. They adjourn to the 9th of January 1660. signed John Hay.

At Peebles the 9th of January 1660.
This day the Justices convened Sir Alex Murray Sir John Veitch the Laird of Stanhope and Mr John Hay of Haystoun. Chuse Haystoun praeses.

This day William Shankland Heard of Lochred complained of John Anderson and his daughter heards of Broughton sheep for committing ryot and striking him and being no otherways to able to prove the same refer it to the defenders oaths who sworn depone negative and are absolved.

In 'summary procedure' it was the practice for people to swear their innocence, hence the 'defenders oaths' when there was no other evidence:

The said John Anderson complained on the said William Shankland for ryot committed by them and also for thiftiously conveying away some of his sheep and smearing and marking the same in his own and other names. He is ordained to have his witnesses ready against the next meeting and both parties to give bond for keeping the peace.

This day the Justices having considered the depositions of witnesses in the cause betwixt Dawick (elder) and the Brouns finds only Patrick Broun son to William Broun guilty of ryot committed upon the person of the said William Veitch of Dawick and they looking on the same as a most presumptious fact being done by such a fellow to the person of a Gentleman of his age and quality Do therefore decern anent the same said fellow to wit they fine him fifty merks scotts to be paid in to the Justices bench and ordain Sir John Veitch to see him carried to East Dawick to the place where he committed the said ryot and there to lie in the stocks eight hours to wit from eight in the morning to four oclock at night and from thenceforth to be banished the parish of Dawick during the said William Veitch his life or pleasure so desires that confinement to be taken and for the future to be bound to the peace and good behaviour to old Dawick and this their act to be put into operation so soon as William Veitch gives bond for keeping the peace as is prescribed by the Act of Parliament for a person of his quality The Justices considering it unjust to punish rigorously any party and yet leave not secured in his person. Dawick refusing to give bond for the peace is ordained to stay within the toun of Peebles till the 23d of January Instant and delivered to a bailie for securing him.

James Hucheon in Skirling complains that George Nicol in Skirling Mains having feed his daughter and she entered home stayed five weeks he had taken her away without any just reason requires him either to take her home to her service or give the entertainment and fee till the time.

The Justices ordain a warrant to be sent to the constable of Skirling to cause the said George Nicol receive home the servant or coming here down before the bench to give a reasonable reason why he will not.

In this last case 'entertainment' was used in the old sense of the word and meant simply the support of the girl during the time she was employed and to repay the fee. The justices were responsible for ensuring that both the master and servant kept to the contract.

In 1660, not long after the death of Cromwell, the monarchy was restored though the everyday lives of people did not change much with the return of the king. The same crimes were committed but it remained to be seen whether the advances made by the justices under Cromwell would survive under a restored Stewart monarchy.

## References


1 APS 1609 cI4 vol iv p434.
2 APS 1587 c57 vol iii p458.
3 Gilbert Hutcheson, *Treatise on the Offices of Justice of the Peace; Constables, Commissioners of Supply with occasional Observations upon other Municipal Jurisdictions* (Edinburgh 1806), vol. 1, p119.
4 APS 1609, c14, vol iv, p434.
5 David Walker, *A Legal History of Scotland* (Edinburgh 1988), vol. 1.
6 P S M Symms, *Social control in a sixteenth century burgh: A study of the burgh court of Selkirk.* Thesis (Edinburgh 1986).
7 Isobel A Milne in *An Introduction to Scottish Legal History* (Edinburgh 1958), vol xx, p352.
8 For example, see the case of Anne, Duchess of Hamilton in *Lanarkshire Minutes of the Justices of the Peace 1707-23,* p25.
9 APS 1587, c57, vol iii, p458.
10 APS 1584, c6, vol iii, p294.
11 A. Whetstone, *Scottish County Government in 18th & 19th Centuries.* (Edinburgh 1981), p39.
12 RPC ix lix
13 APS 1609, vol iv, pp434-5.
14 RPC ix p696.
15 RPC ix pp75-80.
16 RPC viii p624.
17 RPC ix p235.

18 APS 1609, vol iv.
19 RPC ix p409.
20 *Sederunt Book for the Justices of the Peace for the county of Peebles.* SRO JP3/2/1
21 RPC ix p91.
22 RPC ix p714.
23 RPC ii p302.
24 RPC vix lxx viii
25 RPC (second series) viii p326.
26 J Irvine Smith in *An Introduction to Scottish Legal History* ( Edinburgh 1958), p26.
27 APS 1579, c37.
28 Hutcheson, *op. cit*, vol. 1, p49.
29 Symms, *op. cit*, p175.
30 *Ibid.* p119.
31 APS 1617, c8, vol. iv, p535.
32 RPC (second series) xiv pp570-571
33 R Mitchison *A History of Scotland* (London 1982), p.163
34 RPC xi xxxiii
35 APS 1640, c54 vol v, p297.
36 F D Dow, *Cromwellian Scotland* (Edinburgh 1979), p145.
37 CSP Domestic 1655, p139.
38 Hutcheson, *op. cit*, vol 1, p12.

# CHAPTER 3

# *Restoration and Parliamentary Union*

After the accession of Charles II in 1660 parliament passed a commission for justices in 1661 with instructions which effectively removed all evidence of any reforms under Cromwell and put justices back to their original position of the previous decade, leaving only minor changes from their halcyon days. The heritable jurisdictions were reinstated. One instruction particularly affected the justices: the nobility were once again to be outwith the jurisdiction of the justices as were prelates, privy councillors and lords of session. In effect it re-asserted the pre-eminence of the nobility and reduced the judicial status of justices until after the Union.

## *THE NOT PROVEN VERDICT*

It was during the reign of Charles II that the proven and not proven verdicts were first used in Scotland. This was an example of the evolution of the law over time under the influence of major events such as civil war and religious controversy. In this case a significant factor was the reluctance of juries to convict in an atmosphere of religious intolerance which characterised Scotland throughout the 17th century. Hutcheson states that Scottish juries 'exercised of old, the unquestionable power of determining the law as well as the fact' by findings of 'fylit, culpable or convict' if they thought the panel was guilty. If they considered he was innocent, the verdict would be 'clenset, or acquit' or occasionally, 'innocent'. This continued until Cromwellian usurpation, when verdicts of 'clean' and 'guilty' were used.[1]

However, a change in the wording of the indictment occasioned a change in the verdict as juries were asked 'to find the libel proven'. This upheld the other opinion that juries were judges of the facts only and left the judge to deal with the interpretation of this verdict in terms of guilt.[2] Hutcheson comments on the not proven and proven verdicts as being a 'dangerous innovation (which) was promoted and confirmed by the practice then introduced of special indictments'. Hutcheson was not concerned at the style of the verdict but at the change in the powers of the jury.

In 1728, however, after a trial where there was clear evidence of homicide (while aiming his sword at one man the accused kills another) the jury returned a verdict of not guilty. The verdict followed elaborate pleading by the defence, that on the whole circumstances the accused had not committed murder. The verdict of not guilty meant a difference of opinion between the court and the jury. The court could only accept the verdict. Other verdicts of not guilty were made around the same time but in those cases there was no difference of opinion with the judge.[3]

After this the practice was to use the not proven verdict where there was not sufficient lawful evidence but where there was a good deal of suspicion felt against the accused. The verdict does not appear in the early sederunt books for the justices and it would appear to have been used only by juries.

Justices in England were also dealing with repressive religious statutes. 'In 1661 John Bunyan, who as a nonconformist and an advocate of religious liberty, suffered long periods of imprisonment notwithstanding the obvious desire of the J.P.s to show leniency.'[4] Originally sentenced to three months he was not released until 1672, and again imprisoned for two years in 1675. He wrote *The Pilgrim's Progress* while in prison.

### *THE ACT OF 1661*

Justices of the peace in Scotland were reinstated after the restoration in the Act of 1661 which stated 'in all time coming there shall be Justices of His Majesty's Peace' but appointment was yearly and only during the reign of the monarch with a new Commission being engrossed on the succession of the next monarch. To maintain continuity the justices retained their offices for 6 months following the death of a king to give the Privy Council time to re-appoint a commission which may or may not have contained the same names. As already noted, the 1661 Act was based on Cromwell's *Instructions* which had in turn been modelled on the 1617 Act, so in fact little had changed since the advent of the justice of the peace.

The Restoration parliament had passed an act to fine those charged with disloyalty during the Interregnum. This fine was of varying amounts but enforcement was not easy. It was not until 1665 that Charles demanded payment of the fines, but even then he met with little response. He attempted again in 1666 with the inducement that if the first of the two instalments was paid, the second would be remitted. This had the effect of reducing the number of men available as potential members of the Commission of the Peace since so many had lost lands. The same parliament was much more insistent that all citizens with positions of trust should take the declaration, an oath declaring that the National Covenant and the Solemn League and Covenant were unlawful. Sheriffs were to ensure that all justices and magistrates subscribed the oath.

Further acts passed the same year within the justices' jurisdiction included 'an Act against Swearing and excessive Drinking.' Anyone found drunk was to be fined in accordance with his status, that is, each nobleman £20 Scots, each baron 20 merks, each burgess 10 merks, each yeomem 40 shillings, each servant 20 shillings, and each minister in the parish a fifth of their stipend.

There was also an 'Act against Children who Curse or Beat their Parents' which was punishable by death. It is not recorded how often this was used, but it is indicative of what was considered worthy of the death penalty in Scotland compared to England, which, however, had substantially more capital crimes than Scotland throughout its history.

The practice of penal transportation began in 1648 when for the first time justices required to sign orders for the transportation of 'vagabonds' to the colonies. This was virtually a licence to allow ship owners to transport prisoners to America to work on the plantations. Prisoners and vagabonds had to be willing to go to Barbados or Virginia but it is not difficult to imagine how they were persuaded. The choice was the 'chance to serve the country' or execution. A supplication in 1666 by James Dunbar a 'merchant bounding for Barbados' stated:

> Out of zeal for his country and promoting of trade and the credit of Scotsmen in the foreign plantations, he has by warrant of the Justices of the Peace seized several vagabonds and idle persons to carry to the said plantations; and seeing there are several prisons in Edinburgh, Canongate, Leith and other places content to give their own accord and therefore he craves as follows. The Lords authorise Justices of the Peace to apprehend vagabonds and to deliver them to the petitioner for transport to the Barbados; and ordain the magistrates of Edinburgh, Leith and Canongate to deliver to him such persons as are willing to go to Barbados, the Lord Justice clerk being first aquainted therewith and his consent procured.[5]

The return of the heritable jurisdictions meant that the justices were prised from their recently acquired position within the legal system. Coupled with this was the loss of jurisdiction over the great lords and magnates, so that the prestige of the office dwindled and fewer men were willing to take on the burden. The result was that in 1683 the Privy Council had to threaten to punish anyone who refused a commission. In a further attempt to encourage the justices, an Act of 1685 allowed them to keep the fines they imposed but this was short-lived as the Act was rescinded five years later.

In 1667 the Commissions of Supply were established. This was a serious threat to the justices since the commissioners took over the collection of Land Tax, previously an important function of the justices. Since gentlemen preferred to be commissioners of supply rather than justices of the peace, a further Act was passed compelling men to take both appointments or neither. However, in the 18th century the responsibilities of the Commission of Supply were extended to include tendering for the building of roads and bridges – and these responsibilities were shared with the justices. In the end the Commission of Supply usurped many of the duties of the justices because – despite the two bodies often sharing personnel and functions – it was much easier to call a meeting of the Commission of Supply than the justices since the latter lacked an executive chairman who could call meetings in a crisis. Joint meetings of the two Commissions often took place at the instance of the commissioners of supply. It was through the Commission of Supply that Scottish landowners were able to express their opinions and so create the basis of a county government. The administrative functions of the justices were assumed to a great extent by the Commission of Supply although the justices managed to retain their judicial role. All administrative functions of both the Commission of Supply and the justices of the peace were eventually taken over by the county councils in 1888.

Trade expanded during the 17th century and it was increasingly important to maintain lines of communication. The statutes on the highways of Scotland were particularly concerned with the state of roads between market towns and seaports to encourage as much trade as possible. Bridges were built shortening journeys considerably but lack of civil engineering skills required for road building meant that highways would remain in poor condition until the middle of the 18th century. The justices had powers to convene the necessary labour to repair the roads. Labourers, taken from local estates and farms were bound to give 6 days work per year for three years and to bring their own equipment with them. It was possible for wealthy employers to buy his servants out by paying the justice who could then use the money to hire another labourer.

Scotland in the late 17th century experienced considerable unrest as a result of the continuing pursuit of covenanters by Government forces, the political revolution of 1688 and the civil war which it precipitated, and the four years of famine which closed the century. Lack of good seed grain for the following year and bad weather caused malnutrition, disease, and death all over Europe. This was the first sustained famine for forty years and it came at a time of increasing prosperity and a general rise in the standard of living. It was also a time of growing intellectual vigour, and of achievements in architecture, medicine, and law. Stair's *Institutions of the Law of Scotland* was published in 1681. Despite this codification, corruption in the administration of justice was widespread – the impartiality of Cromwellian courts had vanished with the return of the heritable jurisdictions.

The 1661 Act ordered that the quorum between quarter sessions would be three justices. This meant that there had to be three justices sitting to make any decisions at petty sessions. This must have been extremely inconvenient and was one of the reasons why the son of a justice of the peace would himself be appointed on his 21st birthday. Sessions could take place in any room and were frequently held in the local inn or kirk or even the justices' homes. Petitioners had the right to come to the justices at any time or place to have procedures begun. Any number of justices up to a full quorum appeared at quarter sessions to deal with the administration of the county. The same men also constituted the appeals court when decisions made at petty sessions could be reviewed by way of a retrial. Justices were advised not to sit on their own appeals; though frowned on.it was not illegal.

The way was now open for the justices to be as effective in Scotland as their colleagues in England, if it had not been for the heritable jurisdictions, which thwarted all attempts to improve the situation. The stumbling block for the justices was that their jurisdiction was strictly limited by statute. Parliament added to their burden by increasing their work load in the court.

Few records remain of the work of the justices before the turn of the century other than those from Peebles. From the numerous Acts of Parliament governing them it is evident that there were problems. The *Register of the Privy Council* of 1683 records that many counties requested fresh lists of justices as many were now dead or infirm. However in some counties justices were conscientious; for example, the justices of Midlothian appeared to have been active in trying to mend the roads and had organised a voluntary toll on each road and street to raise money for the upkeep. This commenced in 1683 and requests for the toll to continue were made two years later.

### *UNION OF THE PARLIAMENTS*

In 1707 the two Parliaments were joined in the Treaty of Union which comprised separate Acts of the Scottish and English Parliaments, and contained conditions to keep Scots law and the Scottish Church free and independent. The justices of the peace were reappointed with expressly the same powers as the English but with the proviso 'That in the sessions of the Peace the methods of Tryall and Judgement shall be according to the laws and customs of Scotland.'[6] This nullified the intention of parallel jurisdiction because Scots law decreed that serious crimes should go before superior courts: in effect the Scottish Commission was never to have the jurisdiction enjoyed by the English. Despite the desire of James VII to put an end to the heritable jurisdictions and his frequent Acts of Parliament decrying their 'sloth', he found he could not afford to compensate the barons for the loss of their positions. The Treaty of Union declared that all the heritable jurisdictions should continue as before.

There were several attempts at this time to bring the Scottish Commission of the Peace into line with the English commission as far as possible. Scottish justices were given powers over the new customs and excise regulations now in force in Scotland. These were two quite distinct revenue collecting functions, excise being the duty on goods made in the country and customs the duty on goods brought in from abroad. The jurisdiction of the justice of the peace with customs and excise was to hear any cases brought before him by an officer of the new board.

Scottish quarter sessions were fairly erratic, only the busier courts meeting on the statutory days; it was more convenient to meet on days when other groups convened, such as the Commission of Supply which comprised mainly men who were also justices of the peace.

### *THE QUORUM*

Petty sessions were originally designed to deal with the daily minor crimes committed between sessions and the date and place of these sessions was variable – even to being held in the local kirk. Quarter sessions were decreed to be held at the head town of the area and all justices of the peace were expected to attend although the quorum had been set at three with two forming a quorum for petty sessions.

The quorum was originally a select number of justices chosen for their knowledge of the law, a distinction which had virtually disappeared in England before the commission of the peace was introduced into Scotland and most justices were named 'of the Quorum' which according to Hutcheson 'only expresses the confidence of the crown in the knowledge and attention of *all* the justices.' [7] The Privy Council decided in 1612 that 'Four Justices of the Peace salbe ane full number and session to decyd in maters ocurring betwixt the Four Quarter Sessions.'[8] but there must have been considerable difficulties in gathering four men together for the daily minor actions of the Petty Sessions.

The number of justices sitting on the bench varied from county to county but in 1730 it was held by the court of session that two justices should form a quorum as in England.[9] No single justice could act judicially unless specially authorised by statute, and this was only when signing warrants or taking affidavits.

One of the advantages of appointing the eldest son a justice of the peace when he attained his majority was that it enabled two justices in the same household to be available for daily matters. Many of the justice papers of Alexander Campbell of Barcaldine[10] are signed by both him and his son and are indicative of the petty matters happening on a daily basis. These may appear trivial but were important to the lives of the people concerned – just as justices today deal with the everyday situations vital to the quality of life. Quarter sessions were important as they were simultaneously administrative and judicial meetings for the county. Many aspiring members of parliament were also justices of the peace. The quarter sessions provided a forum for all to air their views.

Should there not be sufficient business to be dealt with on the statutory days the justices were at liberty to adjourn them to a later date within that quarter and hold a general session. Special sessions could be summoned for dealing specifically with the execution of a statute. Special and general sessions were held at a date and place nominated at the time of the adjournment. The clerk of court had no authority to call any meeting other than quarter sessions and could not arrange a meeting even in an emergency. This was a severe disadvantage to the justices, who had no leader or chairman.

Justices had jurisdiction over the whole county although this was divided into districts for easier administration, with each district having its own clerk and fiscal.

### *APPEALS*

Quarter sessions were also appeal courts when the justices of the peace heard appeals from other sessions including the licensing of premises. It was in this situation that the number of the quorum had to be at least three, to prevent the same justices from hearing appeals from their own decisions, which though not illegal was considered improper. Appeals took the form of a re-trial. Often the quarter sessions would refer an appeal to 'a committee of their number to examine, take evidence and report.' [11] There was no appeal to quarter sessions from other quarter sessions. These were dealt with by the circuit court and had to be lodged, with reasons, within ten days of the sentence. Copies had to be given to the other party or his lawyer at least fifteen days prior to the circuit court. The appeal had to be accompanied by enough money to cover the costs.

### *DEDIMUS POTESTATEM*

On the abolition of the Privy Council in 1708 appointments to the bench were issued by the clerk of the crown in chancery on the authority of the Lord Chancellor who could refer names to the secretary of commissions for character references. The clerk of the crown in chancery was then instructed to engross a new Commission for the county which was sent to the sheriff and then delivered to the clerk of the peace who would read it aloud at the first quarter sessions following.

The Commission of the Peace was accompanied by a writ of *Dedimus Potestatem* ('We have given power') issued out of chancery and directed to the justice or justices responsible for administering the qualifying oaths before those new justices took their places on the bench. [12] The Dumfries sederunt books cite several instances of appointments of new justices and mentioning the *Dedimus Potestatem*:

> At Drumfries the 6 day of June 1774 Robert Maxwell Esq. of Cargen present provost of the Burgh of Drumfries accepted the oath of office of Justice of the Peace for the County of Drumfries and gave his oath in terms of the schedule annexed to the Writ of Dedimus and thereafter

> qualified himself for the said office by taking and swearing the Oaths appointed and subscribing the same with assurance.

The *Dedimus Potestatem* accompanied all commissions until 1878 when the Crown Office Act 1877 changed the rules. It was not until 1955 that the Secretary of State for Scotland assumed responsibility for appointing justices.

Justices of the peace were appointed from the landed gentlemen of the area and were expected to have a certain income. This monetary qualification was not as stringently adhered to in Scotland as it was in England. Following the Union commissioners of supply also had a monetary qualification of £100 annual land rent. Simply owning land had sufficed prior to the Union. Strangely enough, there was little prestige to being a commisioner of supply despite the fact that it was probably much more advantageous to the landed gentleman than being a justice. Townsmen were excluded from the Commission of Supply as the Royal Burghs paid their tax separately, although certain officials from the town such as the provost could be commissioners.

### *QUALIFYING FEES*

A fee was payable by the justices when they were appointed. This was to pay the clerk of court for the administrative work involved and to the clerk of the crown in chancery to write the name on the Commission of the Peace. The fee only became payable in Scotland after the Union of the Parliaments in 1707, prior to which it appears to have been waived. This fee had been collected in England since at least the 14th century. The justices of the peace in both Scotland and England were unhappy at being charged this not inconsiderable fee on appointment, and many justices whose names were on the Commission of the Peace chose not to act in protest A considerable number of the Scottish nobility were in penury following the rebellions and famine which affected Scotland over this time: they simply could not pay the fee, and so failed to qualify to act in administering the county.

This fee, which varied slightly depending on the rank of the men concerned, is mentioned in a letter of petition from the Clerk of the Crown and the Secretary of Commissions in 1698:

> setting forth that time out of mind their predecessors have received a fee of £3:19s:10d from every nobleman or Custos Rotulorum in England and Wales made a Justice of the Peace and a fee of £3: 9s: 10d from every

private person of the Quorum and £2:17s:4d if not of the Quorum, having a commission to be sworn.[13]

Evidence of the unhappiness of the Scottish justices at this unsought for burden (a little over £40 Scots) may be found in a letter which Sir Alexander Maxwell wrote in 1712 to the Lord High Commissioner:

> Nothing weakens the administration in Scotland so much as the Commission of the Peace being in the hands of persons not well affected to the Queen's administration and nothing would strengthen the Government more than a new nomination of such persons as are well affected.When application was made to the Lord Chancellor to issue out a new Commission of the Peace for Wigton his Lordship seemed unwilling to leave out any names of those who were in the former commission but allowed a small addition of some that had been left out and the member of Parliament who applied for the same was to be at the charge of the *Dedimus* for which 20 or 30 guineas was to be paid, which will make new commissions difficult to be had seeing private gentlemen will not be at such a charge for the public service. It is hoped your lordship will take the premisses into consideration being of much importance to the support of the government and discouraging persons that are disaffected.[14]

The problem continued for several years and in 1716, John Baird of Newbyth, M.P. for Edinburgh wrote to the Earl of Stanhope that

> the gentlemen heritors of this shire are very uneasy that there is no commission of the peace sent to them for want of which the public business of the shire such as repairing of highways, mending of bridges and etc is whirby at a standstill and even the revenue does suffer by it , because the collector and other officer of the excise during the vacation when the exchequer does not meet have no body to supply to about frauds committed by the brewers and retailers of ale. You know very well where the matter stands and that there were promises made that these commissions should be paid for without burdening the gentlemen who are positively resolved not to consent to be at any charges for the expending this commission because they complain that these dues are innovations these commissions being always *expide gratis* before the

> Union and that the office of Justice of the Peace here instead of being a place of profit as it is in some other places is a considerable burden to the gentlemen that do attend. [15]

The government responded six months later, in December 1716, stating that 'the justices of Scotland need not pay the fees, but the Treasury had to recompense crown officers for the unpaid fees.'[16] These two letters also show the importance of the work of the justice of the peace and just how onerous it was at that time as they performed all the local administration required to run the county.

The fee for the *dedimus potestatem* was payable only the first time the oaths were taken.[17] The payment died out very slowly in Scotland, the last instance noted being in 1966 for Mr Thomas C. Smith J.P. of Moodiesburn in the County of Lanark, who received a letter from the Clerk of the Peace in Hamilton inviting him to take the oaths and stating that 'The statutory fee payable on qualifying is l6/3d'.

The fee was an administrative arrangement. In the 18th and 19th centuries, it was about £4 in England, of which £3: 13s: 6d went to the clerk of the crown, 2s went to the clerk of the peace and the balance to the person who administered the oath. Wages then were paid in fees for work actually carried out. A similar situation was in practice over the border but it varied from county to county. In 1767 an Act allowed justices to take the oaths required only once in the reign of each monarch. Justices were not paid for their services but they were recompensed for any expenses. This request went to the sheriff who either paid it from a county fund or presented it to the exchequer with his own accounts.

The Commission of the Peace was altered fairly frequently and during the first 50 years following the Union there was an amount of political manoeuvering and manipulation of the bench, although packing it with supporters of one political party was not favoured. Despite the fact that many justices failed to qualify themselves to perform the duties of a justice of the peace they still considered it a disgrace to be put out of the Commission. Gentlemen who were willing to serve on the Commission of the Peace were obliged to take the Oath of Allegiance. Many Jacobites found this possible only by adding that the monarch was '*de-facto* if not *de jure.*' This 'conscience calming' was removed with the introduction of the Oath of Abjuration. In England justices were required to produce a certificate confirming that communion had been taken in the Anglican Church and again a fee was payable for this certificate.

Both Scotland and England were experiencing unrest during this time. Politics and the law are inextricably linked and having the ruling classes on the bench made confrontation inevitable. Specific instructions from the Government to 'seize rebels and the disaffected' were ignored and particular leniency was shown to rioters prior to the 1715 rising. The government responded by making a significant increase in the military component of the bench.[18] This was not a popular move and debates ensued as to the value of raising the monetary qualification (which was hardly adhered to in Scotland anyway) from £100 to £200 to prevent such men from having a place on the Commission of the Peace. The problem however tended to be self-perpetuating as justices who had been blatantly subversive and imprisoned or fined often had their estates confiscated and as such were automatically removed from the bench, but this diminishing number of aristocrats created access for those of lesser social status. In many cases the political views of these new justices were unknown and this in turn allowed a number of non-conformists on to the bench who were not afraid to refrain from executing the laws of the government.[19] Before the 1715 Jacobite rising 261 justices were dismissed as suspected Jacobite sympathisers[20] and many others were removed from office afterwards. However 'the evidence suggests that the removal of conspicuously disaffected Tories was being balanced by the inclusion of loyal Whigs in the counties experiencing the most violent upsurges of Jacobite discontent.' [21]

## *CUSTOMS AND EXCISE*

Many taxes, which applied in England prior to the Union but which were not to be imposed on the Scots for several years as part of the Treaty, created trouble when they were finally introduced north of the border. The Scots had a somewhat relaxed attitude to paying customs dues and did not take easily to new taxes. Customs fraud on the part of Scottish merchants occasioned complaints from their English counterparts, and to counteract this, English customs officials were sent to Scotland. Customs officials at ports were moved on a regular basis to try to circumvent any fraud. The government announced in 1725 that the Malt Tax would now be levied in Scotland and like most taxes this affected the poorer members of society. Glasgow magistrates openly expressed opposition creating serious doubts that the laws would be enforced. The magistrates were arrested and taken to Edinburgh to be reprimanded and reminded that their role was to uphold the law. Their places on the bench were taken by justices from Greenock at the request of the Lord Advocate.

A similar situation arose in Edinburgh eleven years later when a smuggler was to be hanged. Smuggling had increased rapidly in Scotland after the Union as duties on goods were negligible prior to this time and evasion of taxes has always elicited public sympathy. The captain of the city guard in Edinburgh, John Porteous, was threatened by the mob which had gathered to watch the execution and he ordered the guard to fire, killing and wounding many people. Porteous was arrested, tried and convicted but was reprieved much to the anger of the mob who seized and hanged him. The Edinburgh magistracy refused to acknowledge the reprieve or to quell the riot, allowing Porteous to be hanged. The Government had little choice but to depose the Council and fine the City of Edinburgh.

These are examples of the many disturbances in Scotland at a time when it was increasingly difficult to find enough loyal men to take the Oath of Allegiance and perform the duties required.

There were fears that men of lesser standing would pay the fee to qualify in order to gain the status of a place on the Commission. This would simply further alienate the office from the people. The low social standing, lack of education, and financial status of many of the Scottish justices resulted in a debate in Parliament in 1731 calling for reform. Little, however, appears to have been done: there were similar complaints in 1747, when the sheriffs' workload was increased and, unlike the English sheriffs, their organisation and efficiency outweighed that of the justices.

It is easy to be critical of the justices but they had great difficulties in carrying out the work they were supposed to do. They had no jurisdiction over any one of greater rank and they received little encouragement.

## References


1. Gilbert Hutcheson, *Treatise on the Offices of Justice of the Peace; Constables, Commissioners of Supply with occasional Observations upon other Municipal Jurisdictions* (Edinburgh 1806), vol. 1, p216.
2. David Hume, *Commentaries on Crime* (Edinburgh 1797), vol. ii, p440.
3. *Ibid.*
4. Thomas Skyrme, *History of the Justices of the Peace* , (Chichester 1991), vol. 1, p232.
5. RPC ii p129.
6. 6 Anne 1707,c6.
7. Hutcheson, *op. cit,* vol. 1, p149.
8. RPC ix p409.
9. Reid v Finlayson 1730, Mor. 7636.
10. SRO GD 170/473/1/8
11. Hutcheson, *op. cit,* vol. 1, p85.
12. *Ibid*, p42.
13. CSP Domestic 1698, p285.
14. Historical Manuscript Commission, Duke of Portland, vol. x, p440.
15. PRO State Papers, 54/12 f41.
16. PRO State Papers, 44/120 f97.
17. Hutcheson, *op. cit,* vol. 1, p48.
18. Elizabeth K Carmichael *The Scottish Commission of the Peace 1707-1760,* unpublished PhD thesis, University of Glasgow 1977,
19. *Ibid.*
20. Michael Lynch, *Scotland: A New History*, (London 1991), p327.
21. Carmichael, *op. cit,*

## CHAPTER 4

# *The 18th Century*

### *PROCEDURE*

The justice was the first resort when there was a criminal act in the neighbourhood. The complainer took the problem to a justice who had it written up as a petition by the clerk of court. The justice would then consider whether the crime was worthy of prosecution and, if so, grant a warrant for the constable to serve on the accused, who would be instructed to come in front of the justices and answer to the charges. After this, depending on the answers, the case would be entered into the Porteous Roll for the coming circuit court. It was also the duty of the justice to cite the witnesses and it was not unusual to cite 20 or more for one trial. There was no limit to the jurisdiction of the justices regarding what type of crime they could commit for trial to the high court as most crimes were heard by a jury. The justices themselves dealt directly with only a small number of criminal cases.

Interestingly enough, much of the civil work done by the justices had been taken over on their own initiative on an extra-statutory basis. For instance, they had to deal with the award of aliment to the mother of an illegitimate child from the father. A hearing was called, again with many witneses who would speak to the history of the relationship and the birth of the child. The father could be ordered to pay not only aliment but the lying-in fees of the mother.

### *HERITABLE JURISDICTIONS*

It was widely believed after the 1745 Jacobite rising that heritable jurisdictions were a threat to the country. As already noted, these were courts granted by the king which could not be revoked other than by an act of parliament. The main courts were the baron courts and courts of regality. Regality courts were exercised by a lord with fairly extensive jurisdiction which in certain areas included the four pleas of the crown. Baron courts, subservient to both sheriff and regality courts, thus had limited jurisdiction but held sessions to try petty matters happening locally, mainly on the estates. The rights to the office could be mortgaged or sold and there were frequent complaints about the courts to the lords of justiciary. The office of sheriff altered greatly in 1747 following the Heritable Jurisdictions Act which provided that in future the sheriff and sheriff deputes should be appointed by the crown although no crown appointments of sheriff were made. Sheriff deputes were to be advocates of three years' experience. However these new sheriff deputes were themselves empowered to appoint substitutes to undertake the bulk of their work thus freeing the deputes to attend the Court of Session in their capacity as advocates and continue in their careers. Many of the sheriff substitutes were not legally trained and it was not until 1818 that it became compulsory for them to have legal qualifications.

The office of sheriff substitute grew in power and authority, assuming much of the criminal jurisdiction of the justice of the peace whose remaining remit now lay in the administration of the highways, wages, prisons, the perennial problem of vagrancy and an increasing workload in customs and excise whose officers were both appointed and sworn in by the justices in the county.

### *VAGRANCY*

Vagrancy was a distinct problem in the early 18th century as shown by the numerous acts of parliament dealing with it. Minutes of justice of the peace sessions of 1749 from various counties show several people banished from the county on penalty of being 'whipt by the common hangman once every month or 14 days through the town ... as often as any of us shall return.' Some volunteered for banishment rather than be tried for crimes of theft and vagrancy. The justices' fiscal brought serious cases to the quarter sessions, the justices then committing the case to the next circuit court for trial. Justices were expected to attend the circuit court in their areas until 1710 when procedural alterations were implemented. Crimes had previously been presented to the circuit court by the Porteous Roll, the list of names and details of offences to be dealt with. The Roll and the attendance of all justices at circuit court were discontinued in 1710. Thereafter justices could delegate one or two of their number to attend the court and cases were brought by written presentment.

Justices in Scotland, unlike their English colleagues, never sat with a jury: serious cases always went to the sheriff and jury or to the high court.

### *BAIL*

Throughout the 18th century suspects were given bail before trial if two people would stand surety that the accused would appear at his trial under penalty of a fairly large sum of money. Following conviction for an offence, two people could stand surety that the accused would not re-offend, again under penalty of a large sum of money. The most common punishment was fining and expenses. Corporal punishment was used, although reserved mainly as a threat for vagrants who returned despite being banished but it does not appear to have been extensively used. Justices set up smaller committees to deal with the considerable administrative work such as new Acts of Parliament which had to be made public and brought to the notice of those affected. Intimations were usually nailed to the market cross.

### *PROCEDURE AT QUARTER SESSIONS*

Quarter sessions began with the reading out of any new Commission of the Peace (occasionally the point at which some justices discovered they were no longer on the Commission.) The justices took their oaths in open court and then went on to swear in the other officers such as the constables, overseers of the roads and highways, and customs and excise.

In England at every quarter session, it was the practice to read out the commission and several statutes of importance, including the Riot Act, acts against popery, the Black Acts (against begging) and acts concerning ale measures and burying in woollen, all of which must have been very time consuming; this practice was not adopted in Scotland. Reports were made to the justices from committees or other meetings held in either administrative or criminal capacity. Some counties read over the minutes of the other districts within their counties to create a uniform solution on matters such as maintenance of the poor, vagrants and weights and measures. Criminal cases were laid before the justices, usually by their procurator fiscal or by an individual with the concurrence of the fiscal. Decisions were made by a vote and justices were able to abstain if they so desired. Private prosecutions were extremely rare and had to be undertaken with the concurrence of the King's Advocate.

### *TEXT BOOKS AND MANUALS*

In 1787 Robert Boyd wrote two very large volumes outlining the powers and jurisdiction of the Scottish justice of the peace, his constables, and the

Commission of Supply. The book includes the justices' duties pertaining to customs and excise and his civil jurisdiction. This was followed some twenty years later by a set of four volumes by Gilbert Hutcheson on the same subject and this was considered to be the standard work on the roles of justices for almost a century until the county councils took over most of the administration work. Hutcheson's four volume manual contains a brief history of the Commission of the Peace and a great many of the Acts of Parliament pertaining to the office including some acts on vagrancy dated 1424 and one on the proclamation of general peace dated 1449. The volumes question the jurisdiction of the single justice of the peace and rely on the decision of the court of session in 1760 ruling that at least two justices were required for a quorum since the office was based on the English quorum of two. In the preface to his book, Hutcheson states:

> In Scotland, indeed, there can be no apology for any gentleman wishing to decline the office, in particular of Justice of the Peace, supposed to be the most difficult and troublesome, as it is the most important. The burdensome part of the English Sessions of the Peace is here almost entirely devolved on the Sheriff, whose office in England is entirely ministerial.

This statement is in direct contrast to that made in a very lengthy letter to the Dumfries quarter sessions in June 1799 by John Maxwell of Broomholm, resigning as a justice of the peace;

> It is now upwards of 40 years since the destitute situation of this part of the country forced me, by accepting to do my best endeavours to supply the want of any Magistrates in this corner to whom the inhabitants could have access to apply for redress of grievances, in so far as the limited powers of Justices of the Peace could admit.

He goes on to complain bitterly that as he was the only justice for a large area, he had to cope with so much work that it took up vast amounts of time and expense. His complaints included the limited powers of the justice of the peace and his inability to deal with the grievances brought to him by the locals. He had resigned thirty years previously but was persuaded to return within a year after a new Commission had been engrossed: the work should then have been less burdensome 'by affording the opportunity to get a Quorum for holding District Courts which likewise promised to obviate the plague of attending to daily and I may say hourly applications.' Other resentments were that the Procurator Fiscal was negligent in his duties in not bringing certain people to trial, and particularly that for the third time he was being sued for wrongeous imprisonment. Despite the High Court absolving him, he was left with the expenses while the accused simply entered himself on the Poor Roll and paid nothing: 'it seemed to mark his [Lordship's] unfavourable disposition towards Gentlemen who serve their Country for nothing and at their own private expense.'

The letter was read out in the court by the clerk and answered by the fiscal who assured the justices that he had done his duty in the cases cited by Mr Maxwell. The clerk then informed the meeting that three other justices had also resigned leaving a large district with no acting justice of the peace.

John Maxwell was a conscientious justice appearing frequently at the sessions in Dumfries, some 30 miles from Langholm where he resided. He was very frustrated by the failings of the office and what would appear to be lack of understanding by the high court of the duties of the justice. The realities of the office were certainly more onerous than Hutcheson had stated. The justice was frequently called on personally by petitioners requiring him to act. In his first letter of resignation of May 1770 Maxwell stated:

> The obligation one comes under by acceptance of the office of justice of peace seems not only to bind to a strict administration of justice betwixt parties, but also to refuse access to none who shall apply for it where the matter is competent. The observance of this rule, situated as I am in a remote corner of the county, is surrounded with an extensive country, deprived of every other acting magistrate, has rendered it an intolerable burden.

Maxwell's home, Broomholm House, stands some two miles from the town of Langholm which gives some idea of the distances people were prepared to travel to bring a grievance before a justice. Maxwell obviously thought a great deal about his resignation and understood the problem he was leaving. However, the five justices sitting resolved to write to the Duke of Buccleugh and to the Duke of Queensberry and Dover to persuade them to have another Commission engrossed and copied the letters to Lieutenant General Douglas

M.P. for the County. The following entry for the Dumfries Sederunt book dated 21st February 1765 gives an idea of the work:

> Sederunt John Goldie of Craigmure and James Ewart of Mullock Esquires. There was an information given in by John Maxwell Procurator Fiscal [*not the same man as described above*] of court Shewing That about Six o'Clock in the Evening of the Nineteenth day of January last one thousand Seven hundred and Sixty five years or upon one or other of the days or nights of the said month or of the month of December immediately preceding, William Johnston Indweller in Moffat in the parish of Moffat and County of Dumfries was attacked in his own dwelling house (where he daily rises and lyes down) by Thomas Tod Merchant in Moffat his Son-in-law, who came up behind the said William Johnstons Back while he was sitting at the fire and catched hold of him by the throat with both his hands and griped and squeezed him the said William Johnston so hard that he had almost choaked him. That immediately upon this the said Thomas Tod striped open the cloath of the said William Johnston and searched for money and found in the pockets of his breeches a large purse in which were contained two smaller purses in one of which small purses were 36 guineas of Gold two half guineas one of which was bended, a Six and thirty shilling piece and a piece of Gold or other hard metal which the said William Johnston got in exchange for halfpence to the amount of Seven Shillings and in the other Small purse there were twenty shillings in Silver — That the said Thomas Tod in a felonious Manner robed the said William Johnston of the said Gold and Silver and then run off leaving the said William Johnston lying on his Back on the floor in a State of Insensibility.
>
> That the said William Johnston when he recovered from the State in which the said Thomas Tod had left him alarmed the Neighbourhood with his Crys and soon thereafter gave in a complaint to James Maxwell of Barncleugh one of your number setting forth the manner in which he had been abused in his own house and robed of his money by the said Thomas Tod, the said Justice there upon granted Warrand for apprehending the said Thomas Tod and incarcerating him in the Tolbooth of Dumfries where he still remains. That from the Declaration emitted by the said William Johnston and the declaration of sundry persons m

the town of Moffat all emitted before John Story Baron Bailey of the Lordships and Estate of Annandale And all — Lodged with the Clerk of the peace for this County , there appears Sufficient Evidence to suspect that the said Thomas Tod is guilty of the foresaid Crimes of Hamesucken and robbery and that he ought to stand tryal for the same. Therefore the Informer Craved to the effect underwritten. (Follows the list of Witnesses for proving the crimes above mentioned) William Johnston Indweller in Moffat in the parish of Moffat and County of Dumfries, John Williamson in Chappel in the parish of [BLANK] and county aforesaid, David Johnston Journeyman Gardiner with Andrew Don Gardiner in Moffat aforesaid, Janet Aitchison servant to Andrew Don Gardiner in Moffat, Andrew Don Gardiner in Moffat, Walter Johnston Wright in Moffat, Peter Aitchison in Moffat, Robert Davidson apprentice to Alexander McNaught Weaver in Moffat, John Moffat son to Archibald Moffat weaver in Moffat, Thomas Jack Labourer in Moffat, Doctor James Hunter Physician in Moffat, Mary Boys wife of John Little farmer and Horsehirer in Moffat, Mr James Hunter Schoolmaster in Moffat, John Johnston Senior Merchant in Moffat , John Johnston Writer in Moffat , Archibald Johnston Merchant in Moffat, John Reid Weaver in Moffat, Thomas Reid Weaver in Moffat, Janet Scott wife to John Reid weaver in Moffat, William Scott Journeyman weaver in Moffat, Grizel Reid Sister to John and Thomas Reids weavers in Moffat, Thomas Amos Indweller in Moffat, John Story Writer in Moffat, Baron Bailie of the Lordships and Estate of Annandale, (Follows the Deliverance on the foregoing Presentment) The Justices of the Peace above named having considered the foregoing presentment with the writings therein mentioned and list of witnesses before insert Find the Crimes of hamesucken and Robbery mentioned in the said presentment relevant points of Dittay and ordain the Clerk of Court to transmitt these presents with the said writings to the Right Honourable the Lord Justice Clerk or His deputes at Edinburgh that the same may be put into the Porteous Roll for the shire of Dumfries to the effect the said Thomas Tod may be prosecuted for the foresaid crimes before the Lords Commissioners of Justiciary or any one or more of thier number at their next Circuit Court to be held at Dumfries in terms of the Act of Parliament. (Signed) James Goldie JP and James Ewart JP and J. Hynd (Clerk).

## *ZENITH OF POWERS*

The mid-18th century witnessed the height of the powers of the justice of the peace. The heritable jurisdictions had been abolished but justice remained summary and local. At the same time there was a decline in the zeal with which many Kirk Sessions pursued 'offenders' corresponding to a general moderation in the outlook of the national church.

Traditionally the Commission of the Peace comprised landowners whose income derived from rents received from tenants and who lived the greater part of the year on their estates. Following the Jacobite rising of 1745 many of the great Highland landowners suffered attainder and exile, and forfeited their property and income. Gradually over the next century, with the growth of industry and cities, the landowning class changed to include those who had acquired rather than inherited a country estate, albeit small and without tenants. The expansion of the class took in bankers, merchants and industrial barons. Wealth gradually became the criterion for a place on the bench rather than the rank or status of the local lord.

It became standard practice to place lawyers on the Commission of the Peace and thus there was a rapid growth in their numbers in the early part of the 18th century. Later the Small Debt Act 1825 prohibited solicitors from acting as justices of the peace, and this situation remained until 1906.[1] This allowed solicitors to act as justices of the peace but only outwith the areas where they practised. Since in many parts of the Highlands it became increasingly difficult to find resident landowners to accept a commission, the appointment was again open to men from a wider spectrum than had at first been envisaged.

Although the English Commission of the Peace consisted predominantly of members of the clergy by the 1584 Act of James VI discussed on page 22, it was still considered to be illegal to appoint ministers to the bench in Scotland. However , the peculiar circumstances of the Highlands necessitated the use of ministers despite some resentment that they were of lesser social standing and more often than not, of different religious persuasion from the local aristocrats. It remained unusual in southern Scotland to appoint ministers and indeed was still held to be illegal in 1750, prompting the comment: 'being a man of the gospel he was by law disqualified from being a Justice of the Peace.' [2]

### *INDUSTRY AND INTEREST*

Many Acts of Parliament controlled the rapidly expanding factories and mines, the woollen, linen and cotton industries and various other trades. It was expressly forbidden that justices who had an interest in these businesses should deal with any matters under these acts. A similar situation existed in the coastal areas where justices who were also excise officers were not allowed to deal judicially with cases involving excise. The chief magistrate of each burgh was appointed a justice of the peace as long as he was not a brewer. Personal interest banned men from office.

### *CONTEMPT OF COURT*

The only jurisdiction allowed where a personal interest could be declared was where a justice had been assaulted or insulted as regards his office or in cases of contempt, but it was felt to be preferable if another justice could deal with the matter. Justices were always accountable, but since a convicted person could bear a grudge and accuse the justices of acting wrongly, there were strict rules laid down for suing for damages for wrongeous imprisonment. However the letter from John Maxwell in 1799, mentioned earlier suggests that it was perhaps easier in theory rather than in practice to bring about an action for damages.

The principle was that, unless the justice had acted maliciously, he should not be blamed for acting illegally. Damages were awarded against the procurator fiscal 'whose business it was to know the law and to prevent any irregularity' in a case in the Dean of Guild Court in 1798.[3]

### *SENTENCING*

The powers of the justices regarding punishment of offenders was very limited compared with their English counterparts and they appeared in fact to be reasonably lenient. They were advised in every pertinent act, 'to fine and punish with regards to the quality of the crime and and the means of the offender.' Imprisonment was rarely used before the second half of the 19th century otherwise than prior to conviction or to concentrate the mind and inspire payment of fines. Political prisoners and debtors or those accused of witchcraft could be incarcerated for long periods. Banishment from the county or corporal punishment was common, particularly for vagrancy. Those banished were on pain of being whipped should they return, but both whipping and imprisonment were expensive methods of dealing with offenders. Whipping entailed paying the militia to keep order while magistrates of burghs and justices were responsible for the upkeep of the town jail. To encourage the maintenance of security, magistrates and justices were made liable for the debts of any rebels or debtors who escaped.

Fines and expenses were the most common sentences contrasting with the practice of both the English justice of the peace courts and the Scottish High Court where transportation to the colonies was meted out for some crimes which would appear fairly minor by today's standards.

Lord Cockburn in his book *Circuit Journeys* tells us that he sentenced a man to 10 year's transportation for stealing a greatcoat, commenting that 'had he not been sentenced to be transported before he would have gone before the sheriff' instead of being the only circuit indictment for Dumfries in September 1844. Offences such as those aggravated by previous convictions could result in capital punishment. Juries were reluctant to convict on a charge resulting in the death penalty and so it was common for the prosecutor to reduce the charge during the course of the trial. This enabled the court to impose transportation, seven years being the minimum sentence. Sentences meriting incarceration for more than three years resulted in transportation.

The Sederunt Book of the Justices of Dumfries describes a murder which took place there in November of 1750. It gives a very good account of the procedure and the amount of time it must have taken to do all that was required. Langholm is about 30 miles from Dumfries and the journey on horseback and on poor roads must have taken a considerable amount of time.

24th FEBRUARY 1750.
Sederunt Alexander Copland of Collieston & James Maxwell of Barncleugh. There was given to the said Justices of the Peace by John Maxwell their Procurator Fiscal, a Presentment signed by him, Shewing, That upon the fifth day of December last by past, Lancelot Brown, Son to James Brown in Standing Stean was Incarcerated in the prison or Tolbooth in Drumfries, by virtue of a Warrant of Committment given by John Goldie of Craigninie one of His Majestey's Justices of the Peace in and for the said Shire, bearing date the said fifth day of December, last by past Upon an Information, given in to him by me as Procurator Fiscal, Shewing & Informing, That where upon an Information Exhibited to

Mr. John Boston Chamberlain to the Earl of Dalkieth, Baillie of the Regality of Cannoby upon the first day of December last bypast, that a Strangerman had died the said day in the morning in the house of the said James Brown, where he had stayed some days, and that he died of a bleeding, which was alledged to have been occasioned by a Hurt or bruise he had gott on the Wednesday night preceding, from the said James Brown or the same Lancelot Brown his son, And that the said Mr. John Boston upon the second day of December last, took a Precognition upon the said Information, whereby it appears that the said Stranger was called Thomas Scott, and that the said Lancelot Brown and the said James Brown himself and the said stranger were drunking together at the said James Brown's fireside upon the night of the twenty ninth day of November last bypast, being the aforesaid Wednesday night; And that the sd Lancelot Brown laid hold on the Stranger, brought him over the Fire & flung him upon the Settle ; and that there was blood seen about the mouth of the Stranger or his nose, and that he continued blooding at the Nose until he died, which was the Night of the thirtyeth day of the said month of November, last or the morning of the first day of December also last: That it plainly appeared that the said Lancelot Brown was guilty of murdering the Stranger called Thomas Scott at least, that the Bruises the said Lancelot gave him occasioned such a great Flux of Blood from his nose which was the cause of his death and for which the said Lancelot Brown was then in Custody, which precognition is herewith produced containing the declaration of Benjamin Brown, son to James Brown in Standing Stean, Mary Brown wife to John Armstrong Boatman at Bowheim, John Armstrong Boatman in Bowhelm, John Campbell in Ward of Bowhelm, John Armstrong apprentice to Walter Henderson in Standing Stean, Betty Tod spouse to Walter Henderson mason in Standing Stean and Sybil Daigliesh a neighbour of James Brown. All in the Shire of Drumfries

As also there is herewith produced a Declaration under the hands of Doctor Patrick Maxwell at Burnhead and James and John Mowats Surgeons in Langholm dated the third day of December last , Bearing That, at the devine of Sir William Maxwell of Springkell & Mr. John Henderson of Broadholm Justices of His Majesty's Peace and the same Mr. John Boston Chamberlain to the said Earl of Dalkieth, they, the saids Doctor Patrick

Maxwell, and James and John Mowats, went to view and inspect the Corpse of a man lying in Standingstean at Woodhouselees ground who blooded to death there and was thought to come by that hasty death by some violence or hurt with Lancelot Brown, and James Brown his father in the same James Browns house. They did find upon opening the Chist, that the Lungs did strongly adhere on the Right side to the Pleura, but little or no Corruption, and no Blood to be found in them, and but little in the largest Blood Vessels but could discover no Appearance of Violence or Vessels broke, or extravast blood in the Cavity of the Thorax, nor any Corrupt Smells, but when they came to the Stomach found blood to the quantity of a pound or more, and but a little corrupted, but how such a quantity of blood came there was impossible to find out, both from his having been dead three days and the Intestines tending much to putrefaction; but if he had been Subject to any preceeding Blooding which was reported, they did think that by the Scuffle and Strugling with heat of Passion might have put the Blood into a more Violent Motion than ordinary, and by that enlarged whatever ruptured vessels might be and so poured in these contents as they had found in the Stommach, but in every other case quite healthy and lusty. Which declaration is signed by them all at Woodhouselees the said third day of December 1749.

That the said Lancelot Brown is further Criminal Insofar as He broke prison house at Drumfries where he was confined, made his escape furth of the said prison upon the night of the twenty fourth of day of January.

A few names are attached to the declaration of the escape and then the justices 'transmitt the same to the Right Honourable the Lord Justice Clerk or his Depute to the effect the same may be put into the Porteous Roll of this shire in order to be tried before the Lords Commissioners of Justiciary at their Circuit Court to be held at Drumfries in May next in terms of the Act of Parliament.'

## References

1 Justices of the Peace Act 1906 (6 Edw VII c16).
2 Erskine Murray Papers, National Library of Scotland, 5130.
3 William Butler v John Gloag and others 1798 Dec 18.

CHAPTER 5

# *The Justice in Action*

Prior to the Treaty of Union, justices of the peace watched their criminal jurisdiction diminish. Most crime was considered serious and so was dealt with by a sheriff and jury or the circuit court. The growth and organisation of the sheriff court still contrasted sharply with the lack of organisation and leadership on the part of the justices regarding their criminal jurisdiction. They had onerous ministerial duties to contend with. The main problem lay in the fact that justices did not have a chairman who could work independently. It was only at quarter sessions that a praeses or chairman was elected for each meeting. The clerk of court alone was empowered to call those statutory meetings; all other meetings were arranged as adjourned quarter sessions. No one was empowered to call a meeting in cases of emergency.

Few clerks of court or fiscals were required full time and the justices frequently appointed the sheriff court fiscal as their own fiscal although any work performed in the justices' court would be paid from county money. Most of the crimes had to be remitted to the circuit court. There was in fact very little that the justice could deal with completely, that is, from first appearance through to sentencing, and this gave them little encouragement. The point of being a local judge was removed if the sentencer was not also local and frustrated the intention behind the Commission of the Peace which was to deal with offenders in the locality. The justices themselves decided how much work they would perform but as they were expected to act as county administrators, operate as a police force, supervise the collection of customs and excise and sit as judges it is hardly surprising that some evaded their full duties. However many did carry out their fair share of the work and their names appear in the sederunt books time after time.

## *RIOT ACT*

In 1715 a single justice of the peace was given the power to 'read the Riot Act' in times of trouble. Whenever an 'unlawful riotous and tumultuous assembly of more than 12 persons' was gathered, (and all three circumstances had to exist together), a justice was expected to go into or as near to the assembly as possible and calling for silence was to read from the Riot Act saying

> Our Sovereign Lord the King chargeth and commandeth all persons being assembled immediately to disperse themselves and peaceably to depart to their habitation or to their lawful business upon the pains contained in the Act made in the first year of King George for preventing tumultuous and riotous assemblies. God save the King.

Anyone disturbing the justice of the peace while attempting to quell the crowd was guilty of a felony. The justice was to note the time of the reading and if an hour elapsed without the dispersal of the crowd he was to have them seized by calling on the constables, private individuals or even the militia, who would be indemnified should any of the rioters be killed in the ensuing struggle. This Act was to be read at the quarter sessions although this was never the practice in the Scottish sessions.

### *WORK AND WAGES*

Justices of the peace had a duty to fix the wages of farm servants by the Act of 1617, and this was revised annually at the August quarter sessions. The wages were maximum amounts and masters could pay as little as they wanted. In 1708 certain wages were considered by the justices in Lanark and the following decisions made:

> 1. A domestick servant man or inn servant who is able to performe all manner of work relating to husbandry viz. to plow, sow, stack, drive carts and lay on loads, is to have yearly for fee and bounty £24 Scots at Whitesunday and Mertinmass by equall portions in full satisfacione of a years service and no more.
>
> 2. Item, a manservant of younger years, commonly called a half lang, being a domestick servant, is to have yearly for fee and bounty £16 Scots to be payed as aforsaid and no more.
>
> 3. Item, boyes or lads haveing their meat in the house, are to have £8 Scots for a years service for fee and bounty and no more.

4. Item, a strong and sufficient woman servant for barns , byres, shearing, brewing, baking, washing, and other necessary work within and without the house, is to have for fee and bounty £14 Scots for a years service to be payed asforsaid and no more.

5. Item, a lass or young maide is to have £8 Scots for a years service for fee and bounty and no more. [1]

Justices were to ensure that all able-bodied men and women were hired and to imprison any who refused. The Lanarkshire minutes show that some farmers secretly paid good workers more than the maximum.

***THE LINEN INDUSTRY***

One of the main manufacturing industries in 18th century Scotland was linen and this was being produced in increasing amounts. In 1746 the British Linen Company was established at a time when linen was still mainly produced in the workers' homes. By 1760 approximately 12 million yards was produced. Production grew to just over 19 million yards by 1784 and 24 million yards in 1800. A group of trustees appointed and licenced certain persons to oversee the quality of the linen and to stamp it. They also had powers to ensure the justices carried out their duty to ensure the application of the regulations. Failure to perform their duties adequately could result in the trustees taking the justices and magistrates to the court of justiciary.

The rules were very strict and covered every aspect of linen production from flax growing to the wheels used for spinning through to the finished article. Makers of spinning wheels were also subject to restrictions and had to mark their full name and residence on the wheel before it was sold. The wheel itself had to be to a specific standard. Justices were to deal with any transgression at all points during the manufacture. Servants of dealers in lint seed were expected to tell the authorities if their masters did not obey all the laws and the justices could have the servants imprisoned if they refused. How often this happened is not recorded. A weaver setting up as a master had to give security before a justice of the peace or a magistrate in a burgh, to weave according to all the various laws involved. The manufacturing laws included details like the following: any dyed yarn had to be of sufficient quality to hold in the wash; linen whitened with bleaching agents such as lime, pigeons dung or soap dregs was illegal.

The industry was vitally important to Scotland's economy and a great deal was done to try to preserve it. The leather and woollen industries were also subjected to copious legislation along the same lines as the linen trade. Manufacturing industries were extended greatly during the 19th century and justices had many duties to carry out in regard to this.

Justices of the 18th century had a duty not only to ensure the laws were upheld but also to ensure that the laws were known throughout the shire. In September of 1773 twenty-two justices of the peace met at quarter sessions in Dumfries and appointed a committee to discuss problems within the manufacture of linen with special regard to maintaining the quality.

> The Justices of the Peace appoint a committee of the Praeses Mr Ferguson of Craigdarroch, Mr Goldie of Craigneuk, Sir William Maxwell of Springkell, and John Maxwell of Broomholm or any three of them to draw up an Advertisement reciting the clauses in the Acts of Parliament against False Reeling and False Tale of Yarn in time coming and Enjoining the people employed in Spinning to comply with those Acts in all time coming under the penaltys presented by the said Acts:
>
> At Drumfries the seventeenth day of September in the year one thousand seven hundred and seventy three. Whereas the Justices of the Peace for the County of Drumfries have received information that sundry people in the said county particularly in Annandale employed to spin yarn, do, in violation of the several Acts of Parliament made for the encouragement of the Linnen manufacture, make use of Reels different from those directed by the said Acts and do also make up the said yarn when spun by them in Hesps or Hanks short in the Tale and not containing the number of threeds required by law – The justices assembled this day in their Quarter Sessions held by adjournment, did therefor appoint publick Intimation to be made upon the Church doors of the respective parishes in the said County and at the several Mercat crosses within the same, That they are resolved according to their duty to put the said acts in execution and that no person may have it in their power to pretend ignorance of the same. They notify to all and sundry whom it may concern That by an Act made in the Thirteenth Year of His Majesty King George the First It is enacted that no person shall sell or expose to sale any Linnen Yarn other than such as hath been made into Cutts and Hesps or Hanks each Hesp or Hank

> consisting of Twelve Cutts and each Cutt containing One Hundred and Twenty threeds and no more; and all yarn contained in the Hesps or hanks shall be Lint Yarn only, or Tow yarn only and of the same colour and fineness; and no Tow Yarn and Lint Yarn shall be mixed together in one Hank; and the same shall be tied up with Pack Threed and not Yarn; and the Yarn shall be well reeled and the uniform Standard Reel of Scotland shall be two yards and a half in circumference; and all persons who shall sell or expose to sale or carry from one part of Scotland to another any Lint or Hemp Yarn made up in any other manner, and shall be convicted shall forfeit the Hank made up of fewer Cutts, or in which any Cutt shall be falsely made up, to the Informer: And that it shall be lawfull for any Justice of the Peace or Magistrate within any Burrough or for any person authorised by warrand from them to enter into any House, the doors being open, at all times of the day; and if any Reel be there found other than two yards and a half in circumference it shall be carried before such Justice or Magistrate, who are required to destroy the same, and that it shall be lawfull for the officers herein mentioned at all times of the day to enter into any warehouses, Rooms, Cellars and other places made use of for keeping or making any Linnen Yarn, and seize all such Linnen Yarn as they shall find made up contrary to the direction before mentioned, and detain the same until it be tried whether such yarn be made contrary to the said Act; and if any person shall obstruct the officers from entering such places, or in seizing or carrying away such Linnen yarn he shall forfeit the sum of Five pounds – And by another Act of Parliament made in the twenty fourth year of King George the Second it is enacted That all persons who shall make, sell, expose to sale or buy any Reel not of the dimensions prescribed by the Act before recited shall, over and above the forfeiting such Reel, forfeit such a sum not exceeding Forty Shillings; And all persons convicted of false Reeling and making up or exposing to Sale, selling, or buying Yarn of the produce of Scotland, knowing the same to be Reeled or made up contrary to the directions of the said Act shall, over and above the forfeiting of such yarn, forfeit a Sum not exceeding Ten Shillings, not less than Two Shillings for every Spyndle thereof and so proportionally.[2]

It is interesting to note that all new legislation was to be published on the market cross and church doors to ensure the maximum numbers of people would be in a position to understand it. This was particularly important while the manufacturing of linen remained within the homes of the weavers.

### *SCOTTISH LIEUTENANCY*

There was no permanent Lieutenancy in Scotland prior to the Union. The nobles had relied on personal retainers during any emergencies . Following the Union there were requests from certain areas in Scotland to have a militia but this was met with opposition from the government, who had little reason to have faith in the loyalty of the Scots. Justices of the peace frequently requested that a militia be set up. In Dumfries at the adjourned quarter sessions on 20th of September 1775 the Sederunt Book reads:

> On the ninth day of September current a letter from His Majesty's Advocate addressed to the Sheriff Deputy of this Shire, bearing dates the 4th current, desiring a Meeting of the Justices of the Peace for the said Shire might be called in order to have their aid in putting a stop to the Emigration of His Majesty's subjects and to the exportation of Arms, Ammunition & etc to America, having been laid before such of the said Justices as reside in the Burgh of Dumfries, They appointed the Clerk to write to all the other Justices residing in the County desiring them to meet here this day for the purposes mentioned in the aforesaid Letter: And the Clerk having accordingly sent Letters as directed the following Gentlemen met in consequence thereof.

As only seven justices met and a full meeting had been scheduled for 3rd October they would adjourn until then. They did not actually hold the meeting until the 31st October 1775 when 15 Justices and 10 Commissioners of Supply and freeholders were present. (The letter was sent to 80 justices and cost £1 5s and the reply to the King cost 5s 8d.) The entry continues:

> The Gentlemen before named unanimously resolved that an humble Address should be made out and presented to His Majesty Touching on the State of His Majesty's Dominions in America, and the following Address was made out and unanimously agreed to and signed by the Praeses in prescence & by appointment of the meeting and the Terms thereof follows "Most Gracious Sovereign, We, Your Majesty's most loyal & dutitul Subjects the Justices of Peace, freeholders &

Commissioners of Supply for the Shire of Dumfries in Quarter Sessions assembled humbly beg leave to approach Your Throne with earnest Assurance of our Steady Attachment to Your Majesty's person & Government And firm resolution to Support the Honour & Dignity of your Crown and the Constitution of your Country against all open & disguised Enemys.

We have with Indignation & abhorrence beheld a Set of factious Men in Your Majesty's American Dominions, endeavouring to set in opposition the Legislative & executive part of the Constitution And under the pretext of Grants derived from the one to claim Absolution from their Allegiance due to other while they endeavour to assert principles so totally subversive of sound government by force of Arms. We cannot look on the profession they make of Reverence to your Majesty in Any other light than as empty Sounds and we consider them as equally Enemies to your Majesty, the Liberty of their fellow subjects and the Peace and tranquillity of the British Empire

Actuated by these sentiments we conceive it our indispensable Duty to exert every Effort to protect your Majesty's Sacred person to re-establish peace & Concord throughout the British Empire to give Vigour & Energy to the operation of Law, And to assert & Vindicate that System of Government that has been handed down to us by our ancestors.

In the present Crisis We must lament that this part of Great Britain in which we live is destitute of the Internal Defense which a well regulated Militia would produce. Had we been possessed of such a Safeguard to your Majesty's government and the Liberty & Tranquillity of the country The Military force that may be proper for our security might have operated against the Enemies of Your Majesty in every part of your Dominions.

That your Majesty may be long preserved to disappoint the Designs of your open and secret enemies, that you may transmitt to your posterity the British Empire undivided and Secured by that excellent Constitution by which it has hitherto been cemented and that your Majesty's family may continue to the End of time to reign over a free and happy people is the earnest wish of ...............

It is signed by the Praeses and ordered to be sent to the Member of Parliament and presented to the King. The 'vain sounds' mentioned are in fact the beginnings of the American War of Independence, which had rumbled on for some time prior to this. Revolution in France brought requests from the government for a Scottish militia. However it was not until 1797 that a Scottish Militia was established, amid violent opposition, as the Scots people did not want to be part of a militia which might have been used to maintain the depleted army in America..

The militia was organised by the Lord Lieutenant of the county who was selected from among the greatest landowners in the area. This caused problems since many of them lived in London most of the time. Eventually it was decided that a vice-lieutenant could be appointed from among the deputy lieutenants already *in situ*. The deputies were the men who performed most of the work in the county and had to be justices of the peace – an assurance of loyalty and allegiance. It was not easy to attract men to serve in the militia as many felt they would be forced to join the regular army and end up fighting in France or elswhere. Over the years the military role of the lieutenancy gradually diminished. The Lord Lieutenant as the local representative of the King continued to recommend names of prospective justices of the peace

Many families in the Highlands had their land confiscated by the government after the '45 and further to their dismay tartan was proscribed between 1746 and 1782 as it was considered to be military dress. It seems ironical that the government wanted justices to stop the mass emigration to America but transported nearly a thousand there following the rising. However during this time of proscription, tartan was still produced and exported to America and other countries. Justices of the peace in Stirling were requested during January of 1763 to appoint inspectors to ensure that the cloth was of standard quality so that foreign markets would not be disappointed.[3]

## *CUSTOMS AND EXCISE*

The government encouraged the justices in their jurisdiction over customs and excise. Officers were appointed who were to bring cases to the justices. Customs duties included the administration of oaths to customs officers and commissioners by two justices of the peace. A single justice had power to punish anyone caught removing goods from the shore or buying or selling contraband or 'any suspicious person lurking within 5 miles of the coast with no good explanation.'[4] This jurisdiction was remitted to the exchequer court when large amounts of liquor, over sixty gallons, were unlawfully imported.

Excise duties involved checking the taxes due on goods had been paid, the term goods signifying almost everything – alcohol, meat, sugar, tobacco, coffee, chocolate, printed silks, and linens, glass, paper (which was further taxed after printing), starch, candles, soap and many other products. Most of these excise dues were paid by the manufacturer; if they were caught evading the duty they could be dealt with by two justices.

Originally when excise was first introduced into Scotland in 1644 magistrates of burghs and elders in the countryside appointed collectors of this tax, but in 1803, when new levies were introduced, these were brought under the management of the Commissioners of Excise. Contraventions were dealt with by justices of the peace. One provision was notable: a smuggler with a complaint against the officers had to take it to a higher court and not to a justice of the peace, with whom he might possibly be acquainted. Since it was considered that the jurisdiction of the justices with regard to excise was comparable to English law, there was no appeal to the quarter sessions. Sentences mainly awarded a statutory penalty, and were not reviewable where the procedings had been carried out in a lawful manner. Excise prosecutions were at the instance of an officer of the board rather than the fiscal.

Strict legislation ensured that no one connected with excise, for example, innkeepers or brewers, should act as justices in matters relating to excise. This was also the case with justices who had an interest in any business which came before the courts. As the 18th century saw a tremendous and continual upsurge in manufacturing trade and an increase in the number of justices from these businesses, the various pieces of legislation all laid down very firmly that no interested justice of the peace should act in any matter concerning his own business or indeed that of a close relative.

Robert Burns in his capacity as excise officer in Dumfries wrote out the sentence of the court for a certain Robert Moore: 'I intimate to you that by the decreet of the Justices of the peace for the County of Dumfries you are fined in the sum of £1 stg for making bricks without entry.' It continues 'if not paid within the space of 14 days you will incur the additional expence of 2d on each ls stg. It is dated 26th October 1789 and signed *Robert Burns*.

Informers were paid out of the fines imposed, no doubt to encourage others to come forward. In order to reduce the chances of foreign competition manufacturers and those skilled workers within the trades were prohibited from leaving the British dominions nor to allow any tools or equipment nor information about the skill to go abroad. The penalties for these crimes were very severe at £500 and 12 months imprisonment for a first offence; the justices committed suspects for trial at the circuit court.

The work of the justices varied greatly throughout the 18th century. The sederunt books of the justices of the peace over Scotland during that time reveal the amazing diversity of decisions they made. The following examples are from the Dumfries sederunt books dated between 1740 and 1800. The cases give a picture of life in the 18th century and some of the hardships endured by the people. The Dumfries books record scores of cases where the accused choose to be banished rather than face the court. Banishment was always on pain of whipping should they return.

### *Vagrancy*

On the 6th July 1772 a committee formed by the previous Quarter Sessions, presented their report on the problems of vagrancy. In the ordinary courthouse of Dumfries 31 men, justices of the peace and commissioners of supply met to discuss the contents of the report.

> notwithstanding the former Acts of the Justices and the Publick Laws of the Kingdom this country in general and this county in particular from its situation on the Border and the Regulations established in the Shire of Air and as they are informed, in other neighbouring Shires continue to be oppressed by numbers of strolling poor and licentious vagrants and Gypsies who do not only ask but even extort charity from the country people living at a distance from neighbours and are become in their numbers and boldness an intolerable Grievance receiving under false Pretences that charity which belongs to and should only be bestowed on the Needy and Distressed, who, from this cause are left without the means of support in the parish wherein they reside this taken from them by these sturdy beggars and vagrants. – The meeting do therefore hereby renew the former acts made by them about sturdy beggars and also Enact and ordain that all person or persons who that hereafter be found begging out of the Parish where they have resided for the last three years (which

> is by law declared to be their place of residence) should be apprehended and incarcerated in the Tolbooth at Drumfries as if they were beggars and vagrants not belonging to this County; and the constables are to be paid for apprehending and incarcerating such persons in the manner prescribed by the former acts now renewed by the Justices of the peace and Commissioners of Supply now convened do hereby Enact that every parish within this county be liable to maintain all poor persons who have for the past three years resided in such parish and are in consequence of such Residence to be considered as parishioners and they do further hereby ordain That all constables be active in putting the former acts and this present act in execution, with Certification to such of them as shall presume to neglect so to do That they will be Fined as mentioned in the said acts and they Recommend to the Procurator Fiscal of court to proceed against them accordingly as he shall receive Information from time to time.

The act passed by the meeting was to be published and sent to every justice of the peace and commissioner of supply in the shire and also to every minister of the Gospel so that no one could be in ignorance of the act.

Some twenty years previously the justices had decided that travelling people, called 'Tinkers or Braziers' should have a licence: 'the Justices being of opinion that it is necessary to allow some of these people to travel for the Service of the County have resolved that any Brazier who has a settled residence within the Shire upon his applying to the General Quarter sessions producing proper certificates of his character and finding caution for his good behaviour to the satisfaction of the courts shall get a licence allowing him to travel through the shire about his employment by himself alone.' Those without licences were to be 'deemed vagrants and punished as such.'

***Licensing of Premises***

Four justices were in court on the 1st November 1773 to hear the request from a solicitor that certain premises should be granted a license.

> Andrew Rome in Ruthwell, John Chalmers in Footmanbridge, James Carruthers in Mousewall and John Thomson in Cummertrees conform to written mandates signed by them and addressed to me (the Procurator Fiscal Francis Maxwell).

> Any person keeping an alehouse, tippling house, Victualling house or place of Sale of Ale or other excisable liquors by Retail situated upon or near to the Kings Military Road or Roads made or to be made in that part of Great Britain called Scotland at the publick charge and not being within any Royal Burgh nor within certain Burrows therein mentioned nor within one mile of any Royal Burgh is and shall be intitled to, and the Justices of the Peace for the respective shires of Stewartry and their clerks where such Road or Roads shall and may lye are bound to grant or cause their clerks grant subscribe and deliver to the persons residing on such Roads a Licence in terms foresaid, upon payment of One Shilling for such licence to the Clerk of the Peace of such Shire or Stewartry for his trouble only anything formerly contained on the contrary notwithstanding.

The entry goes on to say that these four men had been to great trouble and expense in supporting and quartering the military

> a burden which in all probability will be also laid upon them for the future. That as this Road on which the persons above named my constituents do live and reside is in every sense a Military road made and conducted by the military at the Publick expense and leading betwixt Scotland, England and Ireland and the different ports and Garrisons thereto belonging; Therefore in terms of the Statute above recited they apprehend themselves well intitled to licences; And I as being authorized by the said Andrew Rome, John Chalmers, James Carruthers and John Thomson do now demand and require of you the said Justices of the Peace and the said Samuel Clark, as Clerk to the peace aforesaid, a Licence for each of the said persons for payment of one shilling sterling for each Licence to continue till the month of November one thousand seven hundred and seventy four and which sums amounting to Four Shillings sterling I now offer instantly to pay; and in case of your refusal to grant such Licences after such offer being made as aforesaid, I, as procurator authorised as aforesaid for the persons above named do hereby protest that they may be free of all trouble or expense concerning the promises and of all the consequences of your wrongeous Refusal now or in time coming, and that the protest may be upheld as equivalent to Licences in favour of my said constituents. And thereupon I require Instruments under the hand of Thomas Stothart Notary Publick and deliver you this schedule this first

day of November one thousand seven hundred and seventy three years before those witnesses James Twadell writer in Drumfries, John Dongan officer there. (signed thus) Fras. Maxwell.

To which it was answered by the Praeses and Clerk of the meeting that the protesters are not intitled to the licences requested in regard that although a military road is made from the Portpatrick to the Burgh of Drumfries and is begun and making from the said burgh through Locharmoss which is about 3 or 4 miles in this county and though it is expected and hoped that the said road will be carried on and finished through this county, yet it is not known in what direction the same will be conducted, nor indeed, whether it will really be completed or carried further: And at any rate that part of it made or begun to be made in this county is not yet near any of the protesters dwelling houses, being above two miles from the protester James Carruthers and above five miles from all the Houses of the other protesters; and none of the protesters have as yet had any of the burden of the military employed on the said Road:

Wherefore the Clerk declined accepting the Fees offered until the merits of the claim made by the Protesters be advised by the court. And the Justices of the peace before named Recommended it to James Twadell Deputy Solicitor of the Stamp Duty, who was present in Court, without delay to transmit a copy or Extract of the aforesaid schedule of protest and answer thereto to Sir James Stewart Solicitor for the Stamp Duty in order to have his direction therein.

***Concealment of Pregnancy and Child Murder***

On 21st February 1767 the complaint of John D Maxwell Procurator Fiscal was laid before the court. Three justices presided, namely Ebenezer Young, James Ewart and John Goldie. The complaint read:

That in the night betwixt Tuesday the twenty fifth and Wednesday the twenty sixth days of November last in the year of 1766, or upon one or other of the days or nights of that month or of the month of October preceding or December following Margaret Douglas servant to John Scoon in Netherthorniewhats in the Parish of Cannonbie and County of Drumfries was delivered of a female child in the house of the said John

Scoon. That she concealed her pregnancy during the whole space and did not call for assistance at the birth and the child was amissing till search being made by order of the Justices of the Peace for this county, upon an information having been presented to them by the Minister and Elders of the said Parish of Cannonbie, the said child was found buried in a barn of the possession of the said John Scoon in Thorniewhats aforesaid.

That the said Margaret Douglas being apprehended by virtue of the warrand from John Maxwell of Broomholm and John Craigie at Langholm Castle Chamberlain to His Grace the Duke of Buccleugh two of her Majesty's Justices of the Peace for the said County she emitted a Declaration before them acknowledging that at the time aforesaid she was delivered of the said Child bye her Masters Fireside , and that the said John Scoon (who was the Father of the Child) acted the part of Midwife and that early the next morning the said John Scoon buried the said child in his own barn by the side of the walls. That the two Justices of the Peace before named upon the Childs body being discovered , buried as aforesaid appointed James Mowat and James Scott two surgeons in the neighbourhood to examinc the body of the Child and report their opinion what were the marks of the child being murdered , or if the same had been born dead; and the two surgeons having inspected the said Child Reported as their opinion That the Child might have come alive into the world and among other things found that the Bone Atlas which turns in the socket of the back of the Head to be very loose and half disjointed and found that the navel String had been cut away from the belly but never ty'd. From those circumstances occurring in the course of a precognition taken before the said Justices they granted warrand to apprehend the said Margaret Douglas and John Scoon and to imprison them in the tolbooth of Drumfries where they now are At least time and place foresaid the said Margaret Douglas being with Child concealed her pregnancy during the whole space and called nor for nor made use of the Help in the birth; and the Child being amissing till found buried as aforesaid the said Margaret Douglas and the said John Scoon are guilty actors or art and part in the murder of the said Female Child. May it therefore please your Honours to find the aforesaid Crime of Child Murder a Relevant point of Dittay and to appoint the Clerk of Court to transmit

> this presentment, Informations, Declarations, Precognitions, and Report herein referred to, to the Right Honourable the Lord Justice Clerk and His deputys that the same may be put into the Porteous Roll for the County of Drumfries to the effect the said Margaret Douglas and John Scoon may be prosecuted for the aforesaid Crime before the Lords Commissioners of Justiciary or any one or more of their number at their next Circuit Court to be held by them at Drumfries in terms of the Act of Parliament.
>
> subscribed John Maxwell

A list of 31 witnesses follows including the two justices who ordered the warrant. The justices found the crimes mentioned a relevant point of dittay and all three then subscribed these proceedings in the sederunt book.

*Aliment of an Illegitimate Child 1778*

One case which took a considerable length of time to resolve concerned the illegitimate child of Elizabeth Renwick and Adam Armstrong. The case began in the kirk session and was then sent to the justices.

> To the Honourable Commissioners in the Peace for the County of Drumfries and Shire and more immediately to John Maxwell of Broomholm Esq. one of the commissioners for the Peace for the said County.
>
> The Humble petition of Elizabeth Renwick Daughter of Charles Renwick of the Grain near Woodhouselees most humbly sheweth That your Petitioner has had the misfortune to be pregnant of a Bastard Child to one Adam Armstrong of the Garden in Cannonby, your Petitioner being summonsed to the Kirk Session there filiated the child according to the order of that Kirk and the said Adam Armstrong was summonsed there also and there did not deny the Child but made some frivolous excuses as differing from the time your petitioner mentioned in the Kirk Session of the childs being got from which objections the Kirk Sessions seems to have no more power or at least passes from it and as your Petitioner is well assured of the Justices of their charge would have the man brought to justice as your Petitioner further observes, she is informed by some that he is advised by some evil designing persons to swear for the Child

and as he has made a confession before the Kirk Session whither or not with Submission should not the tendering him the oath be done with caution until his Objections be Cleared up-which will in a few weeks come out in the truth of it and if the Justice of the Peace should think proper not to tender the oath as it will appear from concurring evidence he is wrong may not the Justice oblige him to give Bail to answer afterwards, if his Objections prove invalid Therefore if your Honour Pleases to consider the above Petition in its variable Circumstances and grant your warrant to bring the same Adam Armstrong before your Honour, or some other of His Majesty's Justices of the Peace to be examined in the said premises and dealt with as the law requires in such cases – and your Petitioner shall pray etc. etc. etc.

signed Elizabeth (her mark) Renwick.

Broomholm 12th October 1778 grants warrant to: Constables and assistants to apprehend the within named Adam Armstrong and to bring him before any Justice of the peace for the county of Drumfries for examination, and otherways to be dealt with as accords to law.

signed John Maxwell JP.

Broomholm 14 October 1778

David Elliot in Hairlawhill Constable having produced the Person of the above mentioned Adam Armstrong and the Complainer being also present the said Adam Armstrong upon examination denys that he is the father of the Child mentioned and the Petitioner offering several times to prove by Witnesses several circumstances which she apprehends will be found relavant to fix the filiation of the Child upon the Prisoner, and agreed that a day might be assigned and warrant granted for Summoning Witnesses for that effect. – We hereby appoint Saturday the seventeenth current at Lymiecleugh at 12 o'clock in the forenoon for proceeding in the matter and ordain all partys to attend accordingly against the said day of adjournment of place and time aforesaid and further grant Warrant in common form to summons all such witnesses as may be needfull for giving evidence in the said matter.

signed Wm Maxwell JP. John Maxwell JP.

Lymiecleugh October 17th 1778

Present Sir William Maxwell of Springkell. John Maxwell of Broomholm Esq. two of His Majesty's Justices of the Peace for the County of Dumfries in the Process depending at the instance of Elizabeth Renwick against Adam Armstrong.

Compeared the said Adam Armstrong who being examined acknowledges that he had Carnal knowledge of the said Elizabeth Renwick for the first time the day preceding the hiring day at Langholm at Martinmass last and the last time some weeks thereafter, but denys that he is the father of the Child of which he stands charged as the Birth of the said Child does not correspond with the times above mentioned. signed Adam Armstrong -Wm H Maxwell JP. John Maxwell JP.

Compeared James Dixon in Archerback a witness adduced for the Pursuer who having been solemnly sworn purged of partial counsel and examined Depones that sometime before Whitsunday last he was told by the Defender Adam Armstrong that he had been with the Pursuer on the night of the Carlisle Fair in August 1777 and that he also told the Deponent that he had lain with the Pursuer but did not mention any particular time or times *Causa scientiae patet* and this is truth as he shall answer to God. signed James Dixon.– Wm H Maxwell JP. John Maxwell JP.

Compeared John Little Blacksmith in Hairlawhill who being solemnly sworn and examined *ut supra*.The Defender Adam Armstrong objected to the above designed John Little giving his evidence alledging that the said Little had told sundry people that he would thrash him the Defender, and on that account he apprehended that the said John Little is an *inhabile* witness which objection the Justices having considered together with the purgation of the witness, They in respect thereof admit him to give his evidence. signed Wm Maxwell JP. John Maxwell JP. and the said John Little being accordingly examined Depones that towards the latter end of Harvest he was asked by the Defender Adam Armstrong if he thought Elizabeth Renwick was with Child and that he acknowledged to him the Deponent that he had lain with her, but that if she was with Child it could not be to him unless it came within a certain time as that the first time that he had lain with her was at the time of Carlisle Fair in August 1777. Depones that about Martinmass last the Defender Adam Armstrong told him that he wondered the Pursuer Elizabeth Renwick ever spoke to him for that he had lain with her twenty times and had promised to Marry her. Depones that on the night of Carlisle Fair in August 1777 he saw the Pursuer and Defender together at the Barrowscrofts kiln and that they went out together and were absent some time and that then it was about ten o'clock at night and this is truth as he shall answer to God. signed John Little Wm Maxwell. John Maxwell

Thomas Armstrong in Barrowscrofts a witness adduced for the Pursuer who being solemnly sworn *ut supra* and examined Depones that the Pursuer was his servant in Harvest 1777 and that on the night of Carlisle Fair in August 1777 he heard a noise in his house and to the best of his knowledge heard the Defender's voice in the bed with the Pursuer and that some days thereafter he was told by the Defender that it was one o'clock in the morning when he the Deponent returned home. Depones that on September 1777 he heard the Defender call the Petitioner out of his house under Cloud of Night and that they went into the Byre together, and that he the Deponent having followed to observe what they were about he heard the Defender say to the Pursuer that he would get her with Child that night and from what immediately after happened in the Byre, to the best of his knowledge, he concluded that they were lying together, tho' it was then so dark that he could see nothing and this is truth as he shall answer to God. signed Thomas Armstrong. Wm Maxwell John Maxwell.

The Justices having considered the above Depositions find the proof therein containes so pregnant with presumption of the guilt of the defender with the Pursuer at the time specified that they find it relevant to intittle the Pursuer to be admitted to make oath in supplement of the said evidence. signed Wm Maxwell John Maxwell.

Compeared the Pursuer Elizabeth Renwick in Grain who having been solemnly sworn and examined Depones that the Defender Adam Armstrong in Hairlawhill is the father of the Bastard Child of which she was delivered on the twenty fifth day of May last, old style, and that the first time that the said Adam Armstrong had Carnal dealings with her was on the night of the fifteenth day of August 1777, old style being the day on which Carlisle Fair happened and that said Adam Armstrong had carnal dealings with her the Deponent at different times towards Martinmass last in and about her masters house at Barrawcrofts – *Causa scientiae patet* and that this is truth as she shall answer to God and depones she cannot write. signed Wm Maxwell John Maxwell.

The Justices having considered the above Depositions find it proven that the said Adam Armstrong is the father of the said Bastard Child and they ordain him to make payment to the said Elizabeth Renwick of the sum of Twenty Shillings Sterling as inlying expences together with four pounds sterling per annum for each year till the child arrive at nine years compleat and further they find the said Elizabeth Renwick is intittled to be custodian of the said child and further they discern and ordain the said Adam Armstrong to make payment of Ten Shillings Sterling to the said Elizabeth Renwick as the expences of this application and Appoint this sentence to be registered in the court books of the Justices of the Peace for the county of Dumfries – signed Wm Maxwell J.P. John Maxwell JP.

### *An Episcopal Pastor Takes the Oaths*

Quarter Sessions of the Peace Held within the Tolbooth of Drumfries the Thirty first day of October one thousand seven hundred and sixty nine years. Sederunt James Ewart of Mullock, John Goldie of Craigmuie and Ebenezer Young of Gulyhill. Mr Goldie Praeses.

Compeared Joseph Messenger Pastor of an Episcopal Meeting in Drumfries who gave in his Letters of Orders in obedience to the Statute in that behalf made to the end they may be recorded as is thereby required And whereof the Tenor follows, 'By the tenor of theses presents We Charles by Divine permission Lord Bishop of Carlisle make it known to all men that upon Sunday the Eleventh day of September in the year of our Lord one thousand seven hundred and sixty eight . We the said Bishop by the assistance of God holding a publick ordination in our Chapell at Rose Castle in the County of Cumberland Have admitted to the holy order of Priesthood according to the rites and ceremonies of the Church of England Our wellbeloved in Christ Joseph Messenger Deacon. And have then and there duly and canonically ordained and promoted to be a priest him the said Joseph Messenger. He having been recommended to us as one of an exemplary Life and virtuous accomplishments and sufficiently versed in the Knowledge of the Holy Scriptures and as such approved of Us and our Examiner, He being moreover furnished with a regular Title to serve the assistant Curacy of Bowness in the county of Cumberland within our Diocese and having first taken the oaths required by Law in this behalf and subscribed the articles specified in the Thirty sixth Canon. In Testimony whereof we have caused our Episcopal Seal to be affixed to these presents. Given at Rose Castle the day and year above written, and in the seventh year of our Consecration.

signed Cha: Carlisle.'

Thereafter the said Joseph Messenger condescended upon the Chapell or Meeting House situated upon the South Eastside of the Street called Lochmabengate of Drumfries where he is to officiate as Pastor foresaid and then He qualified himself by taking the oaths of Allegiance and abjuration and signing the same with the assurance.

***Pricing Corn***

On the 30th October 1770 the quarter sessions were held with three justices, namely John Goldie ,William Welsh and Hugh Lawson . John Goldie was elected praeses.

The Sheriff Substitute laid before the Justices of the Peace an Act passed in the late session of Parliament, intitled, 'An Act for Registering the Prices at which Corn is Sold in the several Countys of Great Britain and the Quantity exported and eimported'; with a Letter, in which it came inclosed addressed to the Sheriff Deputy, from William Cook appointed by the Lords of Treasury to receive the returns of the prices of Corn from the several Countys agreeable to the said Act, which Letter is dated the fifteenth day of September last, desiring that the said Act may be laid before the Justices at their first General or Quarter Sessions to be held after Michaelmass then next that they may fix on the Towns and appoint proper persons to make the returns ; Which Letter also Informs that the Standard Winchester Bushel is only to be had of Mr John Savage in Great Tower Street London; and that such Bushel copper bound and Engraved with the name of the Town and completed for this purpose will cost Four Pounds thirteen shillings and will be alike for all other countys; and when the Justices have fixed the Towns it is desired a Line be directed to Mr Savage acquainting him with the names and how he is to send them down.

Which Act and Letter having been publickly read and considered by the Justices of the Peace for this county now assembled at their Quarter sessions next after Michaelmass last They observed that though, by the seventeenth Article of the Treaty of Union between England and Scotland, it is provided That the same Weights and Measures should be used through the United Kingdom as were then established in England and Standards of Weights and Measures should be kept by those Burrows in Scotland to whom the keeping of the Standard of Weights and Measures then in use there did of special right belong; All which Standards should be sent down to such respect Burrows from the Standards kept in the Exchequer at Westminster subject nevertheless to such Regulations as the Parliament of Great Britain should think fit, and that in consequence thereof weights and Measures werc sent down from the aforesaid Standards to certain Burrows and particularly to the burgh of Dumfries and among others a Winchester Bushell of Brass which yet remains, and which they apprehend may answer the purpose intended as well as any Bushell that could be got from the said Mr John Savage, Yet notwithstanding of the aforesaid Article of the Treaty of Union the weights and Measures in Scotland have continued the same as they were before the Union, and are very different in sundry places, even sometimes within the same county to the great hurt and prejudice of Trade and Commerce. And the said Justices of the Peace further observe That in Scotland there is no such officer as Treasurer of a County nor any publick rates levied, except for the Land Tax and for repairing Bridges and Highways; so that they are at a loss How the persons shall be paid who are named for making the Returns directed by the same Act; However being willing to give all the obedience to the aforesaid Act of Parliament They Did and Hereby Do Nominate Direct and Appoint John Blacklock Merchant and inhabitant within the

Burgh of Drumfries and Robert Johnstone an inhabitant within the Burgh of Annan, both Mercat Towns lying within the County of Drumfries to make weekly Returns of the Prices of Wheat, Rye, Barley, Oats and Beans and of the prices also of that Grain called Beer or Bigg and that weekly until the General or Quarter Sessions to be held by the Justices of the Peace after the Twentyninth day of September in the year one thousand seven hundred and Seventy one, containing an account of the prices at which Wheat, Rye, Barley, Oats, and Beans and that Grain called Beer or Bigg are sold in the said respective Mercat Towns and the Average Prices to the before named William Cook who is commissioned by the Lords of Treasury to receive the same; and that they shall deliver or Transmitt Duplicates of such Returns to the Clerk of the Peace for this County or his Deputy four times in the year to be laid before the Justices of the Peace at their next General or Quarter Sessions assembled as by the aforesaid Act is directed. And that they make such Returns from the aforesaid Standard Brass Bushell kept at Drumfries and from a like Bushell which is supposed to be kept at Annan; And such Returns shall be the average prices of Wheat, Rye, Barley, Oats, and Beans and Beer or Bigg, by the Customary Measures of such respective Mercat and also the average prices by the Standard or Winchester Bushell. And the Justices of the Peace now assembled do Recommend it to the Commissioners of the Land Tax for this County at their next General Meeting to Grant such Allowances to the said John Blacklock and Robert Johnston for their trouble in relation to the promises as they shall think reasonable.

signed by the Praeses John Goldie

***Rape***

At Drumfries the Twenty first day July One thousand seven hundred and seventy four years. Sederunt of the Justices of the Peace for the county of Drumfries. James Stewart of Mulloch, Archibald Malcolm of Hayfield and James Carruthers of Warmamby.

Appeared John Aitken Writer in Drumfries Procurator Fiscal of court who gave in the information and Presentrnent whereof the tenor follows: 21st July 1774. To the Honourable His Majesty's Justices of the Peace for the Shire of Drumfries.

The information and Presentment of John Aitken Procurator Fiscal of the Justice of the Peace Court of the said shire , humbly sheweth That upon Sunday the tenth day of July in this present year One thousand seven hundred and seventy four, when Mary Graham Daughter of John Graham in Hole in the parish of Gratnay and shire aforesaid, a young woman aged about fourteen or fifteen years was herding the cows of John Gass an farmer in Floshland in the parish and shire aforesaid, about two hundred yards from the Post Road between Annan and Carlisle John Cook, soldier in the nineteenth regiment of Foot in Captain Robert Saville's Company at present quartered at Drumfries (the said John Cook being at present a prisoner in the tolbooth of Drumfries) laying aside all regard to the law of God and of this and every other well governed Realm assaulted the said Mary Graham and taking her by the Neck threw her down upon the ground, struck her upon the side of the head and swore to her he would murder her if she cried or said a word, and notwithstanding of her crying to her little Brother who was along with her, being a child betwixt four and five years of age to run and tell the people at Floshland, and all the Cries and Resistance as she could make he the said John Cook then and there forcibly and feloniously did Ravish and carnally know her the said Mary Graham against her will and without her consent whereby she was forcibly deflowered in manifest violation of the Peace of our Sovereign Lord the King and against his crown and Dignity — May it therefore please your worships to find the foresaid information and presentment a relevant Point of Dittay and to Transmitt the same with the List of Witnesses hereto subjoined with the Petition of the said Mary Graham and her father to His Majesty's Justices of the Peace with the warrant thereon and Declarations of the said Mary Graham and John Cook and Precognitions of the witnesses relative thereto, to the Lord Justice Clerk or his Deputys that the same may be inserted in the Porteous Roll for this Shire for the ensuing Circuit Court to be held in Drumfries in Harvest next, and may it please you also to transmitt an application by Robert Hodge Surgeons Mate to the said Nineteenth Regiment to His Majesty's Justices of the Peace with the Declarations on oath in consequence thereof which may give further light into the matter.

signed thus: John Aitken P.F.

Following this is a list of eight witnesses and the deliverance stating that the justices had found it a relevant point of dittay and that the case would go to the Lord Justice Clerk.

***Reset***

The following example records an cross-border offence where goods were stolen in England and reset north of the border. On 21st July 1773 in front of two justices, John Goldie and James Carruthers, the procurator fiscal John Aitken gave information:

> That by the laws of this and every well governed realm Reset of Theft or the receiving or disposing of goods knowing them to be stollen is a crime of heinous nature and severely punishable, Notwithstanding whereof true it is that Andrew Reoch of Priorhill and George Reoch of Grycetail or one or other of them are guilty of the said Crime insofar as in the night betwixt the second and Third of January in the year of one thousand seven hundred and seventy two or in one or other of the days or nights of that month or of the month of December immediately preceding or February immediately following the Shop and House of William Sturdy Shoemaker in Benmont in the Parish of Benmont and county of Cumberland having been broken open and there having been stolen or theftuously away taken out therefrom pair of Mens shoes ready made and finished and another pair the one shoe finished and the other not finished with several hides of Ben leather and two hides ready cured and dressed ; and on the night of the Fourth of February one thousand seven hundred and seventy two or in one or other of the days or nights of that month of January immediately preceding or March immediately following the shop of John Hodgeson of the city of Carlisle having been broken open and there having been stolen out thereof about twenty pair of shoes and two pair of boots; and John Forrest at the back of the Hill in Cumberland and Thomas Douglas in Brampton and his wife and brother all from Cumberland or one or other of them being the person or persons who so stole the said Goods, they the said Andrew Reoch and George Reoch received the said Goods or part thereof from the said John Forrest and Thomas Douglas and his wife and brother or one or other of them soon thereafter knowing the Goods to be stolen And each of them the said Andrew Reoch and George Reoch or one or other of them in the

month of March April or June in the said year one thousand seven hundred and seventy two, at least in Spring or Summer one thousand seven hundred and seventy two sold and disposed of part of the said goods or gear part thereof to another to dispose of for them and part of the goods stollen having particular markings viz, WS JB and certain Stamps by which they are known were found in the dwelling houses and custody of both of them the said Andrew Reoch and George Reoch or one or other of them in the months of December in the year one thousand seven hundred and seventy two or January one thousand seven hundred and seventy three and they can give no satisfying account that they came honestly by them . And he the said George Reoch after he had sold part of the said Leather to Alexander Coulthard Shoemaker in Netherwoodhouse March having heard there was to be a search for Stollen Goods he either went himself or sent the said John Forest to the said Alexander Coulthard and persuaded him to hide the leather. May it please your Worships to find the above Information and presentment a Relevant Point of Dittay and to transmit the same with the List of witnesses hereto subjoined and precognition relative thereto to the Lord Justice Clerk or his Deputes that the same may be ingrossed in the Porteous Roll for the shire of Drumfries for the ensuing Circuit Court of Justiciary to be held in Drumfries in the month of September or October next. Signed thus John Aitken PF.

A list of eight witnesses follows and the deliverance that the justices found the information to be a relevant point of dittay and it would be presented to the Circuit Court

***SIR ALEXANDER CAMPBELL OF BALCALDINE***

Other documents surviving from the late 18th century, are the justice of the peace papers of Sir Alexander Campbell of Barcaldine (1792) which are also a remarkable source of information on both the lives of the ordinary people and the amount of work done by the justice of the peace.

Unto Alexander Campbell Esq. of Barcaldine. One of His Majesty's Justices of the Peace for the county of Argyle.

The Petition of Peter MacIntyre of Ferlochan. Humbly sheweth; That about the beginning of Luncheon a Cow belonging to your petitioner Went over the march upon the Tenants part of the farm. When she was hunted by Seven dogs Set to by a number of children who was then taking Care of the Grass The Cow being in great heart and Heavy with Calf Run before the Dogs with such Vigour down the Hill That she fell over a Large Stone. By the said fall she received so much hurt that she never afterward did eat anything except what was forced down her throat Notwithstanding all our endeavours to save her She died in a very short time thereafter. Therefore; May it please your Honour to answer the premises and Grant warrant to Constables or Sheriff Officers to Summon the parents or Employers of the foresaid children to appear before your Honour upon any day and place your Honour will think proper So is that your petitioner May have redress according to justice. And your petitioner will ever pray.

signed Peter MacIntyre. [5]

Unto Alexander Campbell Esq. of Barcaldine one of His Majesty's Justices of the Peace for the County of Argyle. The Petitioner and Complaint Duncan McIntyre in Killiny Lismore.

Humbly sheweth: That whereas John Black in Craiganich Lismore gave a horse in Exchange for Another horse to your petitioner Friday 14th January Current, and your petitioner gave fourteen Shillings sterling with his horse to said John Black according to paction (i.e. bargain) Notwithstanding of said Bargain the said John Black came to your petitioners house upon Monday thereafter and carried from your petitioners house the horse by force and threatened vengeance agamst your petitioner for offering to keep from him his own horse and abused your Petitioner's wife and daughter by pushing and throwing them down upon stones , when Striving to keep the horse So that your petitioner's wife is in danger of losing her life confined to her bed.

May it therefore please your Honour to consider the premises and grant Warrant to Constables to summon the foresaid John Black and the necessary witnesses to appear before you that justice may be done according to law and your petitioner will pray.

signed Duncan X (his mark) McIntyre

***The Constable's Duties***

The following extract is an account by the constable on how he performed his duties in respect of executing the warrants.

> Upon the 23rd day of February 1792 years I, Alexander McKenzie Constable passed at command of an warrant Granted by Alexander Campbell of Barcaldine one of His Majesty's Justices of the Peace for the County of Argyle upon a petition Dated 22 Currant Raised at the Instance of Captain James Campbell Tacksman of Achnacriebeg and by Virtue thereof Lawfully summoned warned and Charged the also therein named and designed Arch'd MCallum Don MCallum Tenant in Achnacriemor Duncan McCallum and Donald McCallum son of the foresaid Arch'd MCallum resedentars and Indwellers in Achnachriemor Collin Campbell in Union and Duncan Stewart apprentice to Dougald Stewart smith at Craignook also Dugald MCallum son to John MCallum in Achnalea and John MCallum shoemaker in Achnacriemor all to compear before a Justice of Peace Court to be holden at Barcaldine upon Friday the 24th day of February Current in the hour of cause to make answer to the within Petition and Complaint. This I did by delivering a full copy of the said petition and warrant with a just copy of citation to the foresaid Arch'd MCallum, Duncan MCallum Don'd MCallum Collin Campbell and Duncan Stewart all personally apprehended and the like full doubels and short copys of Citations. I left for the said Dugald MCallum in the key hole of the most patent door of his dwelling house at Achnaba and the like I left for the said John MCallum in the key hole in the door of his Dwelling house at Achnacriemor after my knocking after severall knocks at each of said doors as use is because I could not get access to there said respected dwelling houses or get either of them personally apprehended. I also lawfully summoned warned and charged James McKim, Robert McKim, Arch'd McKereach Hugh Ross and John MCallum and Colin Campbell all indwellers in Achnacriemor and Donald McKereach at Connel Ferrie and Donald McTallich Chillis Henderson in Achnacriebeg upon the said 23rd day of February and year foresaid as Evidences to prove the facts of the said petition all personally apprehended which respective full doubels and copys were subscribed by me and bear the date hereof with the names and designations of Collin Campbell residenter and Indweller in Achnacriemor Arch'd McIntyre residenter

and indweller in Barcaldine and Hugh Sinclair Ground Officer at Lachandbeach witnesses present when I served same and hereto with me signing.

Archibald McIntyre Alexander Mackenzie Colin Campbell Witness.[6]

Although the complainer had to go to the justice of the peace to have the case begun, the justice then had to present this to the procurator fiscal who took over the procedings. A case in 1798 where a private complainer had taken his grievance to the justices who then dealt with it without the benefit of the fiscal found the High Court unhappy with the procedings. Justices were to deal with those cases where they felt they could competently make a disposal otherwise the case was entered on the Porteous Roll, which was the list of names of accused, with all witnesses to be heard at the circuit court. Dittay was the old word for indictment. The list of witnesses comprised a large number of people who would give information about the offenders within their respective bounds.

Although the justices of Dumfries seem to have sent most of the cases to the circuit court, the justices of Barcaldine in Argyll disposed of a very serious case at the hearing. The process began on 21st February in 1792 with a complaint to Alexander Campbell JP from Captain Campbell (no relationship noted) that he and his wife, nephew and three of his servants were ambushed, robbed and beaten, particularly the servant William Miller who was not expected to live. Mrs Campbell was pregnant and there was concern over her health. The accused men were tried at Barcaldine two days later and, after the evidence given on oath was heard and the confessions of the parties, they were each fined ten shillings 'for the benefit of the poor of the parish.' They also had to pay the surgeon his fee for attending the victim and to find security for keeping the peace for a year as well as paying the expenses of the process which the justices modified to twenty shillings 'being in full of officers dues', of which five shillings was for copying down the evidence.[7]

***The Clerk of the Court's Duties***

The clerks of court were in very influential positions in the 18th century. Originally the appointment was made by the justices but this arrangement had been short lived and from 1686 it became the duty of the Secretary of

State . The appointment was for life or indeed lives as the extract shows. In 1792 in Dumfries the clerk presented the justices with a

> Commission under the hand of the Henry Dundas one of His Majestys Principal Secretaries of State for Great Britain bearing the date the thirty first of December last, Nominating, constituting and appointing them the said Samuel Clarke and Samuel Clarke Junior, his son, to be clerks to the Justices of the Peace within the said County of Drumfries and hail bounds thereof during all the days of their joint lives, with all the Fees, Emoluments, Casualties and Profits thereto with power to nominate and appoint deputies and substitutes under them in the same office for whom they shall be answereable and to alter and change them at their pleasure and by themselves or the deputies to sit and officiate as Cerks in all meetings of the Justices of Peace at their Quarter Sessions and other particular meetings and Courts holden by them within the same County and to uplift and receive the hail fees and profits of the said Office and to apply the same to their own use and to do, use and exercise all sundry other things which any other clerk to the Justices of Peace in any other County or Shire may lawfully do.

Samuel Clarke, father and son, were to sign the sederunt books for many years.

*SMALL DEBT COURT*

Certain of the justice of the peace courts throughout the 18th century dealt with small debts despite having no legal right to do so and it was not until 1795 that the first Small Debt Act was introduced for a probationary period to deal with sums under '40 poundis Scots'(£3. 8s.8d sterling) to be held monthly. It was estimated that recovery of a debt through legal channels cost approximately three times the amount being pursued so it was decided that a cheaper method of recovery for small debts should be instituted. None of the work performed by the justices in the small debt court was to be committed to the sederunt books in an effort to keep costs low. Some courts ignored this and maintained basic records. The debts excluded any money won at cock matches, horse racing, or any other gaming activity nor did it cover any debt on account of spirituous liquors. The small debt court was so effective and popular that it was made permanent in 1800 and the workload steadily increased. The new act stated that two or more justices should hear and determine cases brought which were to be under £5 sterling. The justices had the same obligations on them as in determining any other legal matter with the emphasis on the proof of the fact or the point of right rather than the moral right of the parties in an effort to maintain stringent legal standards. Throughout Hutcheson's *Treatise on the Justice of the Peace,* this emphasis on the bench acting legally is maintained and there is no suggestion that a lay magistrate should make decisions simply as an arbitrator. Decisions were only made by strict interpretation of the law.

Nairn justices met in March 1805 to discuss the advantages of implementing the Small Debt Act and decided that they would meet as regularly as possible and that the clerk would keep, as an official record, the decree of the court, a copy of which was given to the participants.

One clause in the amended Small Debt Act of 1825 disqualified solicitors from acting as justices of the peace. It has been suggested that this was a mistake and it was meant only to bar them from acting in the small debt court but the wording of the act clearly restricted solicitors from being J.P.s in any court. This was condemned at the time but not repealed until 1906.

The £5 limit to the small debt court remained although the act of 1825 stated that it was to be exclusive of expenses. The £5 figure was equal to one week's wages of an artisan. The parties were not allowed to have lawyers pleading for them nor was any of the evidence to be minuted, in an effort to keep costs as low as possible. One case where the clerk had minuted the proceedings was taken to the court of session and the clerk was fined.

The Royal Commission in 1821 on the courts of the justice of the peace in Scotland was extravagant in its praise for justices and their courts and suggested that the monetary limit to the small debt court be raised. This was not to happen and indeed only 16 years later was overshadowed when the sheriff's small debt court came into operation dealing with sums under £10 sterling. This was a considerable blow to the justices and seemed particularly so considering the success of the small debt court; Glasgow (the district court for the lower ward of Lanark) heard 100 cases weekly while Edinburgh heard 8700 cases in 1821, that is, around 167 each week. It was particularly noted that many cases were settled out of court because of the act and that in some areas, access to the sheriff court was limited. Sheriffs sometimes refused expenses if the applicants could have gone to the justices' court. This civil jurisdiction was still in use in 1955 according to the justice handbook of that year, the limit remaining at £5, but it was very rarely used. There were no written pleadings apart from the summons and no solicitors were allowed to appear for either side presumably still with the same intention of keeping costs down. Two justices formed the court but a single justice could hear the roll of cases and grant decrees against defenders who did not appear.

The justice of the peace constable, governed by the Acts of 1617 and 1661, continued to be the officer who served the summons and cited witnesses for the small debt court and who occasionally acted as bar officer; other than this the powers of the constable waned although it was still competent to appoint them in 1955 and warrants to be a justice of the peace constable were given to inspectors in organisations such as the Scottish Society for the Prevention of Cruelty to Animals and they were sworn in by two justices.

## References


1 Charles A Malcolm, ed. *The Minutes of the Justices of Lanarkshire 1707-1723*, (1931).

2 *Sederunt Book for the Justices of the Peace for Dumfries 1763-79.*

3 John T Dunbar, *The Costume of Scotland* (London 1984), p109.

4 Gilbert Hutcheson, *Treatise on the Offices of Justice of the Peace; Constables, Commissioners of Supply with occasional Observations upon other Municipal Jurisdictions* (Edinburgh 1806), vol. 3, p335.

5 SRO GD 170/473/1/11

6 SRO GD 170/473/1/8/3

7 SRO GD 170/473/1/8

## CHAPTER 6

# *Industrialisation and Social Change*

Procedure had not changed much by 1821 when, after arrest, the prisoner was brought before a justice for examination regarding the offence. The prisoner was first warned that what he said might be used by the prosecution and that he did not require to say anything at all. The declaration was written down, read over to him and signed by him or by the justice if he could not write. Should the justice feel that there were no grounds for detaining the prisoner he could be released immediately; if there were grounds the prisoner would be committed for further examination which would usually be before a sheriff. Most crimes were dealt with by a sheriff or by the circuit court. The original examination might be held in front of one justice but the trial or proof had to be by at least two justices.

### *THE ROYAL COMMISSION OF1821*

The legal systems in both Scotland and England had developed in a somewhat haphazard manner with no obvious co-ordination between the various courts in each jurisdiction. In the early 19th century several bodies, Royal Commissions and Select Committees, investigated the system and their findings where implemented eventually brought about a better defined and more coherent jurisdiction on both sides of the border. As far as lay justice was concerned the Report of the Royal Commission of 1821 noted that, where there were sufficient justices and regular meetings, the duties were 'discharged with an activity and zeal as well as intelligence which render their services highly important to the county.' The report goes on to say that one of the 'chief excellences was that despite much time and effort by the Justices, they received no pecuniary reward.' Public knowledge of this situation increased the respect in which the justices were held the community. The report also noted that life in the cities was quite different from in the country and that 'the paternal character and influence' was lost in the city and suggests that a salaried and permanent justice of the peace be appointed in Glasgow. The Commission did not consider the question of training justices. [1]

This loss of paternalism was a very important point, as the Commission of the Peace relied on its members having local knowledge and an understanding of the community which they served. A great deal was lost in early 19th century England when the 'nouveau riche' assumed those positions formerly held by men who had grown up with a sense of duty towards those who lived in their community and worked on their land.

The report was concerned that the procurator fiscal had no certainty of being paid for his work in instituting the examination and the conduct of the trial, 'particularly when the case is withdrawn from the justices and carried before the Supreme Court'. Even where the justices undertook the preliminary examination there was still no advantage to the procurator fiscal - 'in fact it may have been an inconvenience as it may be legally incorrect through no fault of their own'. Tables of fees for the clerk of the peace and the fiscal were drawn up as part of the report giving the fiscal a guinea for a trial for one day and 10 shillings and 6 pence for subsequent days; 4 shillings for writing out a petition and 6shillings for framing the complaint regardless of length. Other than for trials the fiscal was to be paid 5 shillings for the first hour of work and 2 shillings and 6 pence for every other hour. Clerks were paid in a similar fashion with a scale of fees payable for each duty. The table of fees was to be displayed in the room where the sessions were held.

The Commission also noted the fact that justices awarded aliment to illegitimate children although strictly speaking, they had no jurisdiction in this matter. It had grown with their duty to decide offences against morality and to receive assurance from the parents that these children would not be a burden on the parish. The Commission does not make any comment on this assumed duty. Justices also had jurisdiction over marches of land and to straighten the boundaries, again presumably from their duties regarding the roads of the counties.

Manufacturing industries made unprecedented progress throughout the 19th century and towns grew rapidly to contain the influx of workers who had left the countryside and the security of a lord and his manor for a new social level despite having to live in squalor, filth and destitution and all the inherent problems. The population of these towns grew alarmingly and with only an embryo police force, criminal activity flourished. A Glasgow police force was established in 1800 but it was an expensive matter to run a paid constabulary and many counties were not prepared to meet this expense until the compulsory Police Act of 1857 when forces were established in each county. In an attempt to contain the rising crime rate severe penalties were introduced although little was done initially to raise the standard of living of the poor.

In England over this time there were nearly 300 capital offences, the theory being that any one who was involved in any crime, no matter how petty, was undermining the structure of society as a whole and should not be allowed to live. Property was protected at the cost of human suffering. Scotland had only 50 capital crimes but transportation was used regularly by the High Court for some crimes which today would appear trivial.

A large part of Hutcheson's volumes are concerned with the many acts of parliament pertaining to the manufacturing industries. Legislation encouraging the manufacturing industries can be traced to 1457 during the reign of James II when laws were made to prevent people from spending money on goods from other countries such as lace, and wearing only home products. Over the centuries these 'encouragements' were repeated each time the trades required support.

Competition within these industries was very keen and much of the legislation prevented the removal of tools, machines or any equipment whatsoever which was used in British factories. These trades were closely guarded and no manufacturer could emigrate outwith the 'dominion' for fear of foreign competition. The Act of 5 George II (c27) forbade anyone to leave His Majesty's dominions with his tools with the intention of setting up in opposition to a British manufacturer.[2] Factories were inspected by two justices to oversee strict control of quality and to ensure that the excise stamp was used properly.

Emphasis has been laid on the prevention of crime ever since the first acts governing the justice of the peace when justices were given powers to deal with parties threatening to harm another, the victim first taking the oath to swear that his fears were genuine. Questioning of suspects and witnesses was done by the justices and the convicted would be ordered to find surety to keep the peace. Other suspicious persons were classed as those who 'sleep in the day and wake in the night, people who keep suspicious company or live expensively without sufficient obvious means unless they can give a good account of such means.' Creation of the offence of breach of the peace was a preventive measure to stop a situation getting out of control; it did not designate a specific crime. Anyone scandalizing the government or abusing the officers of justice particularly in the execution of their duties; and 'authors of obscure publications and haunters of alehouses.' The daily lives of people were regulated and ordered to an extent which would be unacceptable today.

One important annual function was 'striking the fiars' when the sheriff and a jury of fifteen men, eight of whom had to be landowners, sat to decide the fiar, or price, of grain for the county. The price of bread was then fixed by the justice with regard to the fiars and giving a reasonable allowance to the baker. Crimes against this were answerable to one justice in small areas and two in larger areas. The fiars were also the basis until 1929 on which the ministers stipend was calculated.

Bridges were built to accommodate the growth in industry, with various acts passed to preserve these during construction or repair, one of which forbade the floating of timber down these rivers during bridge construction. Any timber found on the river would be removed and detained by the justice of the peace who was empowered to fine the owner or to sell the wood at a public auction. Any money remaining after making repairs to the bridge and paying costs was given to the owner.

The justices' powers to settle wages had fallen into disuse as gradually craftsmen gave way to machinery and the act governing wages was repealed in 1813.

Throughout the 18th and 19th centuries Parliament passed laws which were intended to cover the whole of Britain but whose legality north of the border was questioned. Many instances of this are cited in Hutcheson's books, for instance, the validity of the jurisdiction of a single justice. English justices had far greater powers than their Scottish counterparts. One of the questions gone into at length in Hutcheson's books is whether or not justices in Scotland had the power to have offenders whipped. It was considered that this punishment could only be imposed by a judge after a trial by jury. Despite this uncertainty, sentences of whipping were occasionally handed down but, as offenders could banish themselves from the county on pain of the sentence being carried out if they returned, it is more probable that they simply went elsewhere.

Justices occasionally took jurisdiction over matters for which there was no statutory authority, as in the Small Debt Court or, for instance, the award of payment from the father of an illegitimate child. This task arose from their duty of ensuring that such children would not be a burden on the parish and the power to fine those who committed fornication. The Commission of 1821 commented that although justices had no express right to hold small debt courts such a right had been upheld by the 'supreme court in respect of the length of time during which it had existed.' Another example was that Scottish justices, despite not having formal jurisdiction, undertook to control the rates of posting (i.e rates chargeable to travellers changing horses at stages along roads). English justices had no such powers. Midlothian justices fixed the hire of a chaise and two horses travelling post at 9d per mile in 1760. This practice was linked to their jurisdiction over roads, bridges and ferries which they were required to build or maintain with the express purpose of improving travel and communications. It is perhaps surprising that the Government did not acknowledge the dedication and zeal of those justices who did perform their duties properly by increasing their responsibilities. Instead their jurisdiction was reduced.

In 1878 Parliament created a new administrative body called the County Road Trustees which removed responsibility for roads and bridges from the justices. At the same time their customs and excise duties were expanded to cover licensing for the county. Certain excise licenses issued by the commissioners of customs and excise on payment of the duty required a reference from the justice of the peace proving the applicant fit to hold a licence. Before 1845 the Poor Law was administered by the parish ministers and their kirk sessions along with the justices, but in that year the power passed to parochial boards on which justices might serve but only as men of standing in the community and not by virtue of their office as justices.

One of the civil duties of the justices was in the attestation of recruits to the army. At the time clerks of court were not salaried but simply paid for work they did. Occasionally this went wrong as explained in a letter to the justices of the peace of Dumfries dated 31st January 1856. The letter also gives an idea of the relationship between the justices and the clerk.

> Sir,
> I have respectfully to bring under your notice the practice in Dumfries and neighbourhood hitherto pursued by Her Majesties' Justices of the Peace for this county, when attesting recruits who have enlisted in the Army, in employing persons other than the Clerk of the Peace or his Deputes to fill up the attestation with their own handwriting, and thus allowing the duties of the Clerk of the Peace to be performed by, and the

fees fixed by statute to be paid to other persons than the Clerk of Peace.

I need scarcely mention that such a course is not proper, and that a moment's reflection will satisfy that I am right in stating so. As long as I have the honour to fill the office and perform the highly responsible duties of Clerk of the Peace, I do trust that Her Majesties' Justices of the peace for this county will support me and at once refrain from the practice now complained of, and in future allow no one save the Clerk of the Peace or his Deputes to fill up the attestations of recruits and to draw the fees fixed by the statute.

I take this opportunity of thanking you and the other Justices of Peace of the County for the attention uniformly shewn to me, and to apologise for the frequent calls made by me upon your time in discharging the laborious duties of an acting Justice of the Peace and to hope that you will further assist me by carrying out my views on the present occasion.

I have the honour to be, Sir, yours most respectfully, Charles Harkness.

The Clerk of the Peace did not become the official legal assessor until 1888 when the county councils were created. The procurator fiscal was more likely to advise in the court. In fact damages were awarded against the fiscal in a case in 1798 when an illegal warrant for imprisonment was issued. Their Lordships in the High Court commented that the it was 'the business of the fiscal to know the forms of the court, and prevent any irregularity.' [3]

### *REFORM*

The second half of Victoria's reign saw the beginning of serious attempts at civic improvement and social reform. Several large prisons had been built in England and Scotland, including Dartmoor and Perth, to hold prisoners of war and by 1814 nine prisons housed some 45,000 prisoners throughout Britain.[4] Prisoners of war who survived were repatriated by about 1816 and the prisons stood empty until transportation was abolished totally in 1857. This was to create a sudden escalation in the prison population since most criminals had been transported and local prisons held only debtors or political prisoners. Landowners who had previously thought of themselves as the ruling classes now found they had to be elected after county councils were established in 1889. These councils, of course, were only part of the then local government administration, for various autonomous boards – namely school, health and roads – still survived independently of the councils. Justices' duties were increasingly restricted and now comprised limited judicial work and the licensing of premises. In 1908, however, with the Children's Act, they began to deal with criminal cases involving young people under the age of 16 by ordering the parent or guardian to pay damages or costs or requiring them to give surety for their good behaviour without proceeding to the conviction of the child.

Under the Burgh Police Acts of 1892 and 1903 any burgh magistrates could be appointed as police judges to sit in burgh police courts in those areas which had instituted such a court. Their jurisdicton was much the same as the justices' court covering minor breaches of the peace, drunkenness and petty theft among many other minor matters. The court appointed a burgh prosecutor and appeals were to the High Court by way of a stated case. The newly appointed magistrates were simply shown where to sit in the court and left to deal with matters as they saw fit. There was no training and very little information given by way of reading matter. (The justices of the peace at least had handbooks.) However the main difference between the justices and the burgh magistrates and police judges was that only the justices sat as a tribunal. The others sat singly.

The Local Government (Scotland) Act of 1889 transferred all administrative powers and duties performed in quarter, general or petty sessions to the county council. But it was only those specific duties which were transferred and not those which were judicial or performed outside of the sessions. Those that they lost were in the main civil duties including those concerned with weights and measures, gas meters, and the appointment of asylum visitors.

The practice of reading a new commission out in open court at the first quarter sessions after it arrived, was continued at least in theory but it is probable that customs like this, and the reading of the riot act fell into abeyance. Many practices changed over the years in certain areas such as the swearing in of justices. It was customary in Scotland for the clerk of the peace to charge a fee varying from 5s to 10s 6d for the administration of the oath although there was no statutory authority for such a charge.[5] It was illegal to charge this fee from the town rates and, as clerks were not paid a salary, the fee was the only recompense they received. Justices did not require to be sworn in the court, although in those areas where the court was no longer used , the occasion remained formal.

The twentieth century saw many changes in the Commission of the Peace particularly in the selection and training of justices. This was the subject of two Royal Commission Reports, in 1910 and 1948, and four handbooks (Irons 1900, 1937; Thomson 1920; Walker 1931, 'The Green Handbook' in three editions from the Scottish Home and Health Department in 1977 and 1989 and from the Scottish Office in 1999). The setting up of the District Courts Association in 1980 and a number of papers and reports issued between 1973 and 1990 played a part in strengthening the position of the justice of the peace by stressing the importance of selection and training. These included a White Paper in 1973 which preceded the District Courts (Scotland) Act 1975, *Lay Justice?* by Bankowski, Hutton and McManus (1987), which examined the role of the District Court, and two reports by the Scottish Consumer Council in 1990.

Despite the assumption by the County Councils of most of the justices' administrative work in 1889 their judicial role remained, although in Scotland by 1900 it was negligible and what remained consisted of licensing various tradesmen or proprietors of certain premises for which a fee was paid. This was a natural follow-on from their jurisdiction in Customs and Excise and licensing of businesses. Other licences issued by the justice of the peace included those for pawnbrokers, gamedealers, theatres, and dealers in gunpowder. Most of these became the province of the county councils but the justice retained his jurisdiction over licensing of alehouses until 1977.

These licences were a method of guarding against fraud by requiring certain classes of tradesmen to take out a licence for a small fee. This ensured that the holder was of reasonable character and enabled the police to keep a list of those who were engaged in practices which could be a danger to the public, might attract the criminal fraternity or could lead to immoral earnings, for example, the keeping of lodging houses. Licensing allowed inspection of the such premises . These duties frequently required the justices to fix a scale of charges and to ensure the appropriate wages were given.

Throughout this time, the town councils had power to pass bylaws in the area, offences against which were brought to the burgh police court where the bailie adjudicated and where he could find himself deciding on an issue on which he had voted in his capacity as councillor. This anomaly still stands in the case of *ex-officio* or 'councillor justices'.

### *JUVENILES*

In 1906 the property qualification for justices was removed and the way was open for a more representative bench, although this was not fully achieved until 1919. In that year discrimination against women on the bench was abolished. Their part became increasingly important when the juvenile court appeared in 1932; by 1953 such courts were obliged to have at least one man and one woman on the bench.

The Childrens Act of 1908 heralded a different approach to juveniles but it was The Children and Young Persons (Scotland) Act 1932 that really changed the treatment of juveniles. This act differentiated between those who had offended and those who were in need of care and protection. The juvenile court dealt with children between the ages of eight and sixteen. (No child under the age of eight can be guilty of an offence in the eyes of the law.) A child was described as being under 14 years of age while a young person had attained the age of 14 but was under the age of 17. The principle behind the court was to pay regard to the welfare of the child or young person and the words 'sentence' and 'conviction' were not to be spoken or recorded . The words required to be used were 'finding of guilt' and 'order made upon finding of guilt'. The juvenile court also dealt with petitions under the Act governing adoption of children but was required to sit on a separate day or hold a separate session when dealing with adoptions.

In 1932 four counties were ordered to constitute juvenile courts — Ayr, Renfrew, Fife and the county of the City of Aberdeen. In fact it was open to all counties which required a juvenile court to hold one. These courts were run on different lines from the normal courts with the emphasis on informality. The justices who sat on the juvenile court panel were chosen from the body of justices on a triennial basis; any vacancies arising were filled at the following quarter sessions. It was not until 1949 that the age limit of 65 was placed on the members of the juvenile court panel. Even then they were not required to resign until the day before the meeting at which a successor was appointed. The juvenile courts were to be held in a different room or on different days from the ordinary sittings of the court and the accused kept separate from those adults charged with offences. Newspapers were not allowed to identify the juveniles in any way unless ordered to do so by the court or the Secretary of State for Scotland. Three justices constituted the juvenile court, 'of whom so far as is practicable one shall be a man and one shall be a woman'.The court dealt with truancy and charges against children with complaints at the instance of an officer authorised by the Education Authority or the procurator fiscal.

Disposals included parents being fined or ordered to pay expenses, the child committed to an approved school or 'boarded out' with a suitable person. A common disposal for the less serious offences, for example, riding a cycle without lights, was admonition, no doubt in the hope that the experience of appearing in court was a salutory one. In 1953 there were 2,850 young people dealt with in the juvenile courts in Scotland. Juvenile courts were discontinued in 1968 and replaced by the children's hearing system which was based almost entirely on the same principles as the 1932 act, but taking children outside the criminal justice system. The justice of the peace was left with little other than the licensing board and minor crimes.

The number of justices in Scotland in 1947 stood at 6200, more per head of population than in England and Wales. The numbers started to decline in 1949 and dropped over the next four decades to 4500. This number has remained fairly constant for some time. It includes approximately 1700 justices on the supplemental list. The comparatively large number of justices was justified by the authorities 'on the ground that there was a greater need for them to attest documents especially in the more remote areas, than was the case in England.'[6]

Justices continued to have statutory duties in both administrative and judicial functions. The administrative side required the justice to stand between the rights and beliefs of the individual and the law, or simply to be a responsible and trustworthy person helping in a difficult situation.

Apart from the licensing premises for the sale of alcohol the Licensing Court could also grant licences to moneylenders, pawnbrokers and theatres. In 1937 the penalty for performing a new show or play without a licence was a fine not exceeding £10 for every day of offending. Justices had extensive jurisdiction over railways, but it was observed in the 1937 handbook that since many justices were also shareholders in railway companies they were disqualified from acting even with the waiver of the parties involved.[7] Offences under the Railway Act included obstructing workers going about their business on the railways. Anyone defacing toll boards or milestones put up by the railway company was to forfeit £5. Other offences encountered were not shutting gates or refusing to pay toll for the carriage of goods. Disputes as to the amount of tolls were settled by either the sheriff or two justices.

## *ROYAL COMMISSION 1910 AND WOMEN JUSTICES*

In 1919 women were finally allowed to be appointed as justices of the peace under the Sex Disqualification (Removal) Act 1919. This act stated : 'A person shall not be disqualified by sex or marriage from the exercise of any public function, or from being appointed to or holding any civil or judicial office or post, or from entering, or assuming or carrying on any civil profession or vocation or for admission to any incorporated society (whether incorporated by Royal Charter or otherwise) and a person shall not be exempted by sex or marriage from the liability to serve as a juror.' Although women could be elected as councillors in burghs or counties in Scotland they had been specifically barred from being *ex officio* justices even when they were Chairmen of Parish Councils or District Committees, positions which usually carried such *ex officio* justice appointments.

The selection of justices of the peace was by way of recommendation of the Lord Lieutenant to the Lord Chancellor but as a result of a Royal Commission of 1910, advisory committees were instituted in every county to encourage a wider range of men to join the commission . It was not until the end of 1919 that women were appointed justices, although the composition of the bench was to remain male dominated. Efforts to increase the numbers of women on the bench were made but were not particularly successful until the last two decades of the 20th century.

The appointment of women to the bench was a question raised by the 1910 Commission to which all the male respondents answered that they did not think the court was a fitting place for a woman. Only one answered that female justices might be suitable but 'they would have to retire for certain cases.' What these cases might be was not explained! This attitude is not particularly surprising in 1910 when 'ladies' were protected from the seamier side of life, but in the report to the Scottish Home and Health Department in 1988,[8] one potential nominator for the Perth and Kinross justices' experiment admitted that he 'never thought of women for that sort of thing.' The first woman so appointed was Miss Elizabeth Haldane C.H. LL.D. to whom James Thomson dedicated the 1920 justices' handbook. As already noted the part played by women on the bench increased considerably when juvenile courts were established in 1932. In 1995 there were 2028 justices of the peace under the age of seventy, of whom only 560 were women. Requests to advisory committees to increase the number of women on the bench have borne fruit and in 1997 47% of new appointments were women.

## *JURISDICTION OF THE JUSTICES.*

There were many and varied administrative duties for justices throughout the twentieth century. Vaccinations were made compulsory by an Act in 1863 but by a later statute [9] parents or guardians were allowed, within six months of the birth, to make a statutory declaration to a justice of the peace that they believed that the vaccination would be prejudicial to the health of the child. Other duties included the execution of deeds for a blind person or those unable to write.

The Secretary of State required the petition for the licence to practise anatomy to be countersigned by two justices certifying that to their belief the applicant was indeed going to carry on the practice of anatomy. Justices of the peace could hear appeals from anyone unhappy about the billeting of soldiers or airmen and had powers to have the officers moved elsewhere. One other duty which could be dealt with by a single justice was that concerning any man wishing to enlist in the army for twelve years.The justice having first ascertained that 'the man was not under the influence of liquor' cautioned him not to give false answers and recorded his answers to the questions on the attestation paper which was signed by the recruit; the Oath of Allegiance was then administered and the man was deemed to be enlisted as a soldier. A fee of one shilling was paid by the soldier to the justices' clerk for this attestation. (Presumably by the mid-twentieth century the problems experienced by the Dumfries clerk in the previous century had been overcome and the clerk received the fee.)

Justices were required to take affidavits and this was considered one of the most important ministerial duties that he had in the early 20th century and certainly the one most often performed. The justice was not limited by his commission area but could take an affidavit in any part of the United Kingdom. In the event of the imminent death of a witness, justices could be called upon to take his deposition on oath. This required two witnesses , the doctor and the justice sufficed. The justice was to take the deposition in writing and ask the witness what he knew of the matter and also put any further questions by the fiscal or the defence asking at the end if this was all true as he should answer to God. The deposition was then signed.

## *LICENSING COURT*

Two licensing courts existed, one in the burgh and the other in the county. It was the latter which was presided over by the justices with the magistrates sitting in the burgh court. In the county court, which could be divided into districts if necessary, half the members of the board were justices and the other half were county councillors. The number of members of the board was decided by the size of population. The court of appeal which sat one month after the first hearing consisted of the same membership plus three more from each group. The term of office was three years although members were eligible for re-election.

The justices' sederunt books for 1895 in Dumfries make poor reading after the detail of the previous century. Statutory quarter sessions were held but often adjourned. On 7th August 1894 the quarter sessions were held with 12 JPs present and the minutes state:

> Report to be considered at the next meeting.
>
> 26th September: Adjourned Quarter sessions with 6 JPs . Amendment to rules to Savings Bank.
>
> 24th October: Special Sessions with 3 JPs to deal with 1 license to deal in game which was granted.

The 13th November meeting saw the County Licensing Committee sitting with 3 justices:

> the clerk having read the list of members on the Joint Commitee for the several burghs appointed last year and all being eligible for re-appointment it was agreed on the motion of the Chairman to re-appointment them again with the exception that Mr Edmondson should take Lennox's place on the Joint Committee for the Burgh of Dumfries.

They appointed 10 justices to be on the Joint Committee for 4 areas.

> 2nd January 1895:
> Adjourned Quarter Sessions with 11 JPs. The clerk reported that the following appeal had been lodged against the proceedings of the magistrates of the Burgh Court at a recent court (6th Dec 1894) — refusal to grant transfer of an Inn and Hotel Certificate. Defence solicitor present. Appeal refused.

It is interesting to note there are no minutes of the actual procedings, only the decision is recorded. The sederunt books of Peebles dated 1900 are similar, simply stating the facts:

> Accused appeared — Pled Not Guilty — evidence led — found guilty — 15/- of modified penalty — payable within 7 days or imprisonment for 7 days.
>
> Appeared John Knox (Contravention of Dog Licences Act 1887 Sec 8) — pled guilty — 10/- payable within 14 days or 7 days imprisonment.
>
> Complaint against W Hastie for naval desertion — Committed to Naval Custody.

During the Great War of 1914-18 and other periods of conscription there was an increase in the numbers of those who had either deserted or failed to report for military service. All were handed over to military custody by the justices. Justices had no jurisdiction under the first road traffic act, simply entitled the Motor Car Act 1903, a situation which was to change drastically as the car grew in popularity over the 20th century. Justices in Peebles in 1914 complained to the authorities about the small petrol ration allowed since there was such a poor train service. There is no note of the outcome of the complaint.

The sheriff, justices of the peace, burgh magistrates and police magistrates within the burgh had concurrent jurisdiction and where the statute creating the offence prescribed the court in which it was to be tried, that court had concurrent jurisdiction with the sheriff court. If no court was named, the offence had to go before the sheriff. The maximum jurisdiction of the lower courts was a fine of £10 and 60 days imprisonment. The sheriff had universal jurisdiction of summary offences in the sheriffdom. The sheriff and the justices jointly and with the guidance of the crown officers determined which court would deal with certain types of offences.[10]

Until 1901 appointments were cancelled on the death of a monarch but the Demise of the Crown Act provided that commissions were not to be affected and thus allowed justices to continue in office for life — *ad vitam aut culpam.*

In 1949 a residential qualification was imposed which required that justices could not be appointed unless they lived in or within 15 miles of the commission area unless the Lord Chancellor, or later, the Secretary of State, allowed it under special circumstances. The retiral age for justices of the peace was 75 and the supplemental list was created to record names of retired justices who had their duties restricted to signing documents to authenticate a signature. Justices who were also members of a local authority were forbidden to act in cases brought by or against that authority.

### *REMIT TO A HIGHER COURT*

Under the Summary Jurisdiction (Scotland) Act 1908 justices could remit the case to the sheriff court if it became apparent during enquiries or the trial that the offence was in fact outwith their jurisdiction or if the circumstances suggested that the higher court was more suitable. The accused could be remanded in custody for up to 4 days for examination. The prosecutor then arranged with the procurator fiscal for the county for the case to be heard in a competent court.

This power to remit to a higher court remained until 1975, but as justices were doing very little criminal work it is doubtful if it was used often and it is not mentioned in the 1954 handbook despite the fact that the 1908 Act was repeated in the Summary Jurisdiction (Scotland) Act 1954. This was repealed by the Criminal Procedure (Scotland) Act 1975 when both the justice and the sheriff lost the power in summary cases to remit a case to a higher court. However the Criminal Justice (Scotland )Act 1980 gave the sheriff power under solemn procedure to remit to the High Court for sentence where the sheriff considered his sentencing powers were inadequate.

Today in terms of the Criminal Procedure (Scotland ) Act 1995 Section 7(a) and (b) there is a power under summary procedure to commit an accused to prison 'until dealt with according to law' if it appears during the preliminary hearing or the course of the trial that the accused has in fact committed a crime outwith the jurisdiction of the district court. On the very rare occasion that this might happen the case must be dealt with by a higher court, not for sentencing but for trial. Justices must remit a case to the sheriff court where it becomes apparent that an accused is suffering from a mental disorder.

Justices of the peace were protected from actions of damages unless the complainer could prove express malice against him. The 1908 Act widened that protection by adding that there must also have been imprisonment and the conviction quashed before a case could be considered relevant. This was repealed in 1977. Protection of justices, clerks of court and fiscals from being sued is now enshrined in the 1995 Act which states (s.170) again that there has to be imprisonment and malice proved before it is competent to sue.

The county councils took over the administration of the justices' court and paid the salary of the clerk although part of his remuneration continued to come from fees paid by certain authorities or individuals. He was not a county or city official but continued to be appointed for life by the Secretary of State for Scotland. The clerk could appoint any depute clerks required. The justices continued to appoint the fiscal for their court. The Summary Jurisdiction (Scotland) Act 1908 governed the procedure of trials and all summary criminal work of the justices of the peace courts. Quarter sessions could hear appeals from other sessions by way of retrial but this procedure gradually died out and most appeals went by way of stated case to the High Court. Under common law the justices' jurisdiction extended only to those offences where the locus was within the county and within the powers of the court. The Act laid down which statutory offences could be competetly dealt with in the justices' court. These tended to be very minor and even when it was competent to proceed before the justices, many offences were still taken to the sheriff court. The workload of the small debt court also diminished and in 1969 Walker stated 'JP small debt courts now operate only in four counties in Scotland, are little used and this court is of trivial importance.'[11] The justices' small debt courts held in Scotland at this time heard 3500 cases per year compared to 22,000 heard by the sheriff.

## *ROYAL COMMISSION 1948*

A Royal Commission in 1948 set up to look at the position of the justices in Britain reported that Scotland had 6,248 justices (exclusive of *ex-officio* justices) but despite this there was a problem in constituting a court in some areas. Scotland had an excessively high number of justices mainly due to the preference of the Scots for justices to sign documents. By this time the quarter sessions were only held to decide administrative matters such as the dates for holding justice courts and to elect justices to sit on the licensing court. Quarter sessions were held nominally but frequently had no business to transact. The court had powers to sentence up to £10 or 60 days imprisinment. The Royal Commission made the observation that

> in England the increase in the judicial work of justices and the decrease in their administrative duties has led to the view that whilst appointment as a justice is honourable it is not a civic honour but an appointment for judicial purposes. The English conception is not applicable in Scotland.

The appointment of justices in Scotland was viewed more as a political reward than in England. Main recommendations were that a Scottish secretary of commissions should be appointed (although this did not happen until 1955); that a Central Advisory Committee should be set up, that the police should inform the Lord Chancellor of any justice convicted of an offence; and that the retiral age should be 75 although the appointment would remain *ad vitam aut culpam* . It was also desirable that clerks of the peace should keep an account of the number of sittings individual justices made and that those justices who moved residence and could no longer perform the duties should be removed. 'He is being relieved of a duty, not deprived of an honour.' .

The Royal Commission further recommended the formation of an association for justices to create an active body which would aid the justices. 'If even a small proportion of JPs is ineffective the dignity and prestige of the office is inevitably lowered.'

Three of the members of the Royal Commission felt that the Scottish Commission should be abolished as the justices performed so few judicial duties, but the other 11 members disagreed and once more the Scottish Commission of the Peace escaped annihilation. Despite these recommendations there were few developments to the courts before the radical changes brought about in 1975.

In 1953 the total number of persons tried in the justice of the peace courts (not burgh) was 11,089, of whom 2,850 were tried in the juvenile court. This was out of a total of 108,453 persons tried summarily in Scotland. By 1973 the justice of the peace courts dealt with 8,616 cases against 84,643 in the burgh court and 116,714 in the sheriff summary court. The large number of cases in the sheriff court was partly because of the increase in road traffic offences.

# References

1 *Report of the Commissioners Respecting the Courts of Session: Ninth Report on Justice of Peace Court* (1821), Vol. X.

2 Gilbert Hutcheson, *Treatise on the Offices of Justice of the Peace; Constables, Commissioners of Supply with occasional Observations upon other Municipal Jurisdictions* (Edinburgh 1806), vol. iii, p324.

3 Hutcheson, *op. cit*, vol. i, p67; William Butler v John Gloag and Others (December 18th 1798).

4 Joy Cameron, *Prisons and Punishment in Scotland* (Edinburgh 1983).

5 Cleveland Ellis, *Local Government (Scotland) Act 1894* (1912), p145.

6 Thomas Skyrme, *History of the Justices of the Peace* (Chichester 1991), Vol. III, p85.

7 J Irons, *Scottish Justices Manual* (1937), 2nd Edition.

8 J J McManus and J Greenhalgh *The Selection and Training of Lay Justices.*

9 7 Edward VII c.49.

10 *Dumfries County Council v Phym* (1895), 22R, p538.

11 Nigel Walker, *Sentencing in a Rational Society* (London 1969).

CHAPTER 7

# *New Tasks for a New Age*

## *LOCAL GOVERNMENT RE-ORGANISATION 1975*

Scottish local government reorganisation in 1975 meant that the government had an opportunity to review the function and indeed the desirability of lay summary courts and following publication of a Royal Commission Report on Local Government in 1969 and a White Paper in 1973, the district court was recreated. The justices of the peace achieved a fresh and distinct role in the judicial system of Scotland as they could now deal with any offence triable in a court of summary jurisdiction which carried a maximum penalty of up to £100, or 60 days in prison. This created a much wider field of offences which could be brought to the justices' court.

The Districts Courts (Scotland) 1975 Act had a very interesting journey and made several about-turns before reaching the statute books. The working party who were to look at the question of lay justice and how to improve the system comprised the following members: the past and present secretary of commissions; a town and a county clerk; a clerk of the peace; a stipendiary magistrate; a burgh prosecutor; the crown agent; the deputy director of Scottish Courts Administration; a bailie; a justice of the peace; and two members of the criminal justice division of the Scottish Home and Health Department. The reorganisation abolished the burghs and counties and replaced them with 9 region and 3 island areas, comprising 53 districts. The White Paper proposed were that the jurisdiction of the court should be more extensive than the then justice of the peace and burgh courts but not as great as the sheriff summary court and it was envisaged that three or more justices would sit together. Justices were to have training and to accept a commitment to sit at least 24 times in the year the same as their opposite numbers in England. The burgh and justices of the peace courts were amalgamated into what was eventually to be called the district court and which would be financed by the district council. The White Paper expressed the government's desire that lay justice should be continued and strengthened in Scotland, and stated that 'the lay judge brings to the court a practical everyday knowledge of the way of life and social conditions in the local community to which those who appear before him belong, and such knowledge is not less valuable, when decisions have to be made as to the most appropriate method of dealing with offenders than the foundation of legal training possessed by the professional judge'.[1] The Government also felt that the system in Scotland had been lacking in properly trained justices who were experiencing regular court sittings. Training and experience were necessary to maintain standards and to foster a 'judicial approach'. The proposed training was justified if the justices were to have a permanent tenure.

One of the proposals made in the White Paper was that the Lord Advocate should take responsibility for prosecutions in the new court to bring it in line with all other courts and ensure a uniform standard of prosecutions. The burgh prosecutor until 1975 had been an isolated individual, quite outwith the Crown Office and answerable to no one. Large centres of population were to have stipendiary magistrates.

It was thought that the court could be run by Scottish Courts Administration which would put it under the same auspices as the other courts in Scotland, clerked by the sheriff clerk service and financed by central government. The courts were to have power to fine up to £100 or impose a maximum custodial sentence of 60 days, with the power to endorse driving licences where there was statutory obligation, although 'totting up' offences were to appear before the sheriff. Other offences to come under the jurisdiction of the justices as seen by the working party were T.V. licence evasion and housebreaking where the value of the stolen property did not exceed £100. The justices were to have no civil jurisdiction. Appointment of justices should be only by recommendation through the advisory committee to the Secretary of State for Scotland; it was not envisaged that councillors would continue to be justices.

However these were only the proposals of the working party put forward for public consideration and the House of Commons had yet to debate them. Opposition came from the legal profession whose initial complaint was that the justices would have no legal advice available, although later their opposition was directed at the proposal to put lay people on the bench. Generally the reaction to the proposals was favourable. Those in favour pointed out the difficulties of assembling a bench of three at the last minute for custody cases or if a justice took ill and felt that a minimum of two justices should be allowed although the norm would be three. Concern was also expressed about the lack of professional legal advice in the court as sheriff clerks do not have legal training. However about six months later the government announced that the lay summary courts in Scotland would be abolished and the sheriff court expanded to accommodate the extra business. The Law Society of Scotland welcomed the proposal and admitted their concerns about lay judiciary. Many organisations were equally concerned at the abolition of the lay courts in Scotland which had enjoyed a long tradition but before anything could be done a general election was held and a new government came into power only one year before the new districts and regions were to come into being. The new Government announced its intention of retaining a lay judiciary and accepted some of the White Paper proposals.

A new scheme was produced whereby existing burgh magistrates or police judges, justices of the peace and *ex-officio* justices appointed by the local authority were all to sit as justices in the new district court which would remain under local authority control. This scheme brought the following comments:

> The introduction of these changes perhaps betokens a lack of total satisfaction with the pre-existing system and may be seen as a partial compensation to those who argued for the complete abolition of lay justices. However it is clear that the eventual decision to retain lay involvement was more the result of political expediency and pressure of time than of any compelling arguments on the point of principle.[2]

> The opportunity was lost to remove local authority involvement from the administration of justice in Scotland ... and Scotland was left with a system more outdated than the one that Parliament had rejected seven years ago as being no longer suitable for England and Wales.[3]

Justices of the peace remained as individual groups within each local authority with no governing body to bring about national standards. Stipendiary magistrates could be appointed by local authorities where there was a need and they were subsequently appointed in Glasgow.

Historically the greatest changes concerned the introduction of training for justices and the formation of a statutory justices committee in each district;

these have been of immense value in deciding the court rota and training requirements. The committee filled a very large void in the organisation of the justices by ensuring an efficient working partnership between the justices, their chairman and the clerk who could be authorised to call meetings at any time. Sadly, for reasons of simplification, it was decided that it was no longer necessary to have the name of each justice inscribed on the commission. Since the earliest days of the justice of the peace when a justice was appointed the Lord Chancellor and later the Secretary of State signed a fiat authorising the inscription of the name in the commission; the name was then added by hand in the office of the crown in chancery. The commission is now addressed generally and not by name, to those 'who may from time to time hold office as Justices of the Peace'. The 1973 White Paper also suggested the formation of a justices' association along the lines of the Magistrates' Association in England. The District Courts Association was formed in 1980 and has been invaluable in organising training of justices on a national level

### *DISTRICT COURTS (SCOTLAND) ACT 1975*

Although the Act contained many of the proposals in the White Paper there were some variations. The Act of 1975 gave the lay summary court a full role in the judicial system and at last the justice of the peace was assured of training and a legally qualified clerk to advise on the law, and for the first time it was planned to introduce legal aid into their court. The Lord Advocate assumed responsibility for bringing prosecutions to the district court. He appoints all procurators fiscal and all appeals are to be heard by the High Court of Justiciary. Appointment of justices was by recommendation of the advisory committee within each district. Justices were to have a committee to decide the court rota and organise training. This committee was separate from the advisory committee. District councils were given the power to appoint up to one quarter of their members as *ex-officio* justices although the justices' committee decide which justices serve on the bench. Clerks of court were appointed by the district council and for the first time became officials of the council.

### *THE SINGLE BENCH*

One of the most significant historical changes was to the quorum, which had consisted of two justices since 1707: the 1975 Act simply states 'one or and sentence, and nationally, the Scottish justice is the only lay judge who has these powers. The district court was not after all to be run by the Scottish Courts Administration but by the local district council and would have a legally qualified clerk to advise the justices. This readily available legal advice was to prove a great asset to the court. The Summary Jurisdiction (Scotland) Act 1975 framed the procedure in summary courts. Since 1975 the powers of the District Court have been increased to include many motoring offences which could not have been foreseen when the Motor Car Act of 1903 was passed.

The District Court (Scotland) Act 1975 brought back the 18th century title for the court, giving the justice of the peace a new lease of life and a real position in the judicial hierarchy which it had never before achieved and placing lay justice firmly in the hands of local people.

Since 1975 there has been growing public awareness of the justice of the peace and a Consumer Council survey did much to point out the shortcomings in both the appointment system and the training of justices.[4] Substantial changes have been made to the jurisdiction of the district court including the power to award compensation to the victim.[5] This can be for either a quantifiable amount through loss or damage to the victim's property or can be an award by the court for physical or mental anguish sustained by the victim and determined by the presiding justice. This was in fact a return to an ancient Scottish tradition of compensation to restore the victim to the situation prior to the incident.

In 1988 the fiscal fine came into existence: this allows the fiscal to issue a conditional offer to an alleged offender instead of prosecution. This offer included every offence which could competently be prosecuted in the district court excluding certain traffic offences for which a fixed penalty could be offered. The 'fine' was £25 and if the alleged offender pays the fine to the district court no conviction is recorded. The offender pays an initial sum to the clerk of court in acceptance of the offer, while the remainder is paid in instalments of £5. Outstanding instalments can only be requested at means courts or by civil diligence. Imprisonment is not an option. This power of the fiscal was increased in 1996[6] to include variable levels of £25, £50, £75, and £100 fines and to include all offences which could be dealt with in the district court. The number of fiscal fines increased dramatically with a 78% rise in the year following their inception, and concerns were raised about 'cost effective justice' and the types of crimes for which the fiscal fine was rise in the year following their inception, and concerns were raised about 'cost effective justice' and the types of crimes for which the fiscal fine was used. The rise in fiscal fines saw a corresponding drop in the cases being brought to the district court so that the offender was not challenged on his actions and justices could not deal with the case. Concerns were raised that the principles of local justice were being eroded. This situation remains unchanged today.

Other changes to the work of justices of the peace have been an increase in fining powers and the inclusion of motoring offences whereby justices have mandatory powers to endorse licences and can disqualify drivers under the 'totting-up' system when a certain number of penalty points have been accumulated. The introduction of motoring fixed penalties further increased the jurisdiction because under this 'totting up' procedure, anyone due for disqualification because of points added under a fixed penalty must be referred to the district court. Non-payment of these fines is also dealt with in the district court. The Criminal Procedure (Scotland) Act 1995 increased the jurisdiction of the district court by enabling all statutory crimes punishable up to level 4 of the standard scale (currently £2500) to be dealt with by justices of the peace.

In 1985 the commission area of Perth and Kinross decided to adopt a radical new approach to the selection and training of justices. A wider trawl of the public than usual was made and resulted in 105 nominations. These candidates were interviewed and 21 were successful and completed a very intensive 12 week training after which 8 were appointed as justices. The usual practice was to appoint justices before training so this was indeed a radical experiment. The training included lectures, tutorials and a great deal of background reading and the scheme was criticised for being too intensive and legalistic. It was thought by some to dilute the 'layness' of justices. There was to be a fixed term of appointment of 8 years but, after approving such expensive and time consuming training, the authorities were reluctant to lose such valuable assets. Although this experiment has not been repeated in any other area the selection process is now more open and the names of the members of The Justice of the Peace Advisory Committee (JPAC) are now made public. The scheme certainly helped bring about a fresh look at the training of justices. [7]

In 1995 the district court in Scotland dealt with 38% of summary criminal offences while the stipendiary magistrates dealt with 6% and the sheriffs with 56% . The distribution of summary criminal business between the sheriff court and the district court remains much the same. In 1997 the district courts dealt with 36% of summary criminal offences. Only 1% of disposals from the justices' court were prison sentences and the main disposal was fining, with an average fine of £82 in 1996.[8]

Local government re-organisation took place again in 1996 when the regions and districts were abolished and 30 new authorities created. The justices courts were not faced with removal in this re-organisation but once again the chance was lost to put the court under the auspices of the Scottish Courts Service in line with the other two tiers of criminal justice in Scotland. The district court remains under the local authorities and continues to be without uniform standards. This is an anomaly that must be remedied in the near future for the benefit of all involved in the district court. Inititiatives such as the Scottish Justice Charter or Judicial Studies in Scotland do not include the justices as they are not under the same central funding authority.

A typical modern court list will contain speeding or other road traffic offences, assaults, misuse of drugs, breach of the peace, theft and reset, and shop-lifting. Fines remain the main disposal but there is more use of probation and in certain courts, community service orders. Supervised attendance orders are used for those who appear at means enquiry courts but only as an alternative to imprisonment for non-payment of fines.

### *DEVELOPING THE ROLE OF JUSTICES - NEW OPPORTUNITIES*

The story of the Commission of the Peace does not end with the 20th century. It is ever-changing, by necessity, in an ever-changing world and adapts as and when required by parliament to meet the needs of justice. Where the Commission was exported to the Commonwealth it adapted successfully according to the demography and geography of the new country. There is no reason to think that the 21st century should be different. The justice of the peace is a valuable part of the social fabric and administration of criminal justice in the local area and this resource should be used to the full. The participation of the public as lay judges involves a great number of people who would not otherwise be part of the criminal justice system and this in turn increases public awareness of the system. This can only be advantageous in a system which prosecutes in the public interest for members of the public who have been victimised in anyway. As Lord Chancellor Jowitt said in 1948, 'I think it is an excellent thing that justice should be administered by the ordinary lay people.' The Scotland Act 1998 came into force in 1999 and with it the Scottish Parliament, which has power to legislate on a wide scale, although many important matters such as the constitution, defence, national security and employment will continue to be the sole province of the sovereign parliament of the United Kingdom. The Scottish Executive is the government in Scotland in relation to all devolved matters and its members include a First Minister, who appoints junior ministers, the Lord Advocate and the Solicitor General. A Minister for Justice has been appointed for the first time in Scotland.

How much the jurisdiction of the justices of the peace will continue to expand will depend on several factors: the workload on the sheriff court, the co-operation of justices in training, and the desire of the Scottish Parliament to increase the amount of work in the district court. There are several possible ways in which the present limited jurisdiction of the justices could be expanded to the benefit of the public. More specialised training would be necessary but this would merely emulate the situation in England where the justice of the peace deals with 97% of criminal work, as well as family and youth courts. Training is at present organised by the local committee and funded by the local authority but as the workload increases there is an increasing need for training of all justices to a national standard with identified competencies in all aspects of court work. This should not be designed to make quasi-lawyers of justices but to enable justices to have a full understanding of their role and an increased ability to function well in the court. Skills and knowledge of the key areas can only be beneficial to those who pass through the courts. Training is not only for new justices but ongoing for all who are sitting on the bench. After all, the power to deprive offenders of their liberty, the most basic human right, is a very onerous one.

Appointment to the commission of the peace must also be scrutinised and potential justices, while still representing 'all manner of people', must have at least a basic standard of education, and show a willingness to continually update their training. There is no reason why the Scottish justice of the peace should not determine all summary criminal work as in England, relieving the burden on the sheriff courts and freeing sheriffs for civil and solemn business. Scotland has a clear-cut three-tier system of criminal courts and to devolve all summary work on one tier would involve little more than increasing the jurisdiction of the district court to the present sheriff court limit of three months imprisonment for common law offences or six months for second or subsequent offences of dishonesty or personal violence or a fine up to £5000. Statutory offences carry their own maximum fines. A summary jurisdiction of this level would bring the district court to the same limits as English magistrates sitting summarily.

Local courts have to strike the balance between bias through familiarity and the necessary objectivity required to adjudicate 'without fear or favour, affection or ill will.' Local knowledge of the area must not be confused with personal knowledge of an offender. One of the strengths of the justices is that while working within the strict parameters of the law they can bring a knowledge of what will be accepted as legitimate and fair within their local community. 'The rule of law is not subverted by this injection of a lay element. On the contrary, this lay element is necessary for its full and proper working. This is not something sinister but rather the only morally acceptable way a society based upon the rule of law can be organised.'[9]

One problem area which justices of the peace may encounter is that of human rights. The European Convention on Human Rights secures all the rights and freedoms of the individual and was ratified by the United Kingdom Although these rights are not generally enforceable before the courts directly, the view was taken that Parliament intended to legislate in conformity with the Convention and not in conflict with it. The Human Rights Act of 1998 will come into force for the United Kingdom in the year 2000, giving effect to the various articles of the Convention such as the right to life, liberty, security, a right of respect for private and family life and a prohibition of torture and degrading treatment ot punishment. However, Section 29 of the Scotland Act 1998 states that any act of the Scottish Parliament is not law if it is incompatible with any of the Convention rights. Accordingly any acts of the Scottish Executive or public authorities, including the courts, will require to have regard to human rights and any possible violation of these. Possible violations may be signalled by the alleged victim or his solicitor in the course of the proceedings in court but the justice will also require to have regard to violations when considering and granting warrants. In general, every criminal court including the district court, will be able to refer such challenges which arise in their proceedings to the High Court of Justiciary to be determined by that court. These important issues will be part of the law of Scotland considerably before they become UK law in terms of the Human Rights Act 1998.

***Small Claims Court***

As has already been noted, the Justices of the Peace Small Debt (Scotland) Act 1825 established a small debt court to deal with claims of £5 or less. Despite a long passage of time this £5 limit was never increased and the number of cases gradually dwindled well before it was abolished by the District Courts Act 1975. The new small claim procedure did not revive any of the justices' previous powers, since only the sheriff court was empowered to deal with them up to a sum of £750, with a maximum of £75 for expenses if the award exceeds £200. The purpose of introducing the small claim procedure was to try as far as possible to make the court accessible to the public, without the necessity of instructing a lawyer, and with assistance available from court officials to fill in the necessary summonses and other forms. In these circumstances this procedure seems to lend itself to lay participation and some consideration could be given to reviving , particularly in this straightforward manner, the former powers of the justices of the peace to deal with minor civil disputes. This would have the effect of releasing the sheriff court to deal with the already heavy burden of civil litigation, particularly in the expanding area of family law.

The main aim of the court would remain to have the claim settled as cheaply and efficiently as possible. Three justices sitting with a legal assessor would perhaps be less intimidating to the public than the sheriff court. The principles of lay justice apply as well to civil law as to criminal and as 'the District Court is closest to the people whom they serve' it would seem appropriate that small claims should be placed in the hands of the justices.

***Civil Marriages***

Justices of the peace and judges in most States in the USA have the authority to marry couples, a jurisdiction taken to America in the early 17th century. In Britain, civil marriages are held in registry offices which in many cases means a cramped room with little space for guests. We have gone a long way from the days when a registry office wedding was a quiet, hurried affair. Today many couples express the desire to be married in a hotel or a garden or some other place which has a special meaning for them. Registrars are often unwilling or unable to perform these ceremonies, and this leaves the couple with little choice but to opt for a religious ceremony in which they may have little or no belief. Justices could conduct the marriage in the chosen place with all the guests present, a return to the practice instituted by Oliver Cromwell who gave English justices the power to marry couples, having abolished the religious ceremony. In later years in Scotland, when clandestine marriages were popular, although frowned on by the authorities, the justices 'married' couples by fining them for having entered into an illegal contract, and the extract of conviction, handed over on payment of the fine, was accepted as proof of the marriage. Giving justices the power to officiate at marriages would give the couple a wider choice than at the moment and may perhaps in the process help to underpin the institution of marriage itself.

### *Youth Court*

There is a growing need for a court to take those offenders who are too old for the childrens hearing but whose age and offences do not warrant the degree of formality employed in the sheriff court. The district court at present deals with many young people between the ages of 16 and 18 and for many it is their first formal court appearance. It is not uncommon to have a 17-year-old father in court who understandably may object to being called a child, whatever his mental or social capacity. Adolescents face a multitude of problems — peer group pressure, unemployment, a growing drug and alcohol culture and related issues of 'growing up'. There is a great deal of debate about the age at which juveniles should be dealt with in court, and whether there should be a specific cut-off point at 16. A Youth Court could deal with adolescents and young people up to the age of 21 and might combine the features of both the hearing system and the adult court by giving equal importance to the interests of the youth and of the public.

It is acknowledged that making a personal appearance in court can be effective with young people in accentuating the seriousness with which society views the offence. Special training in youth court work would enable justices to deal effectively with a growing number of offenders. The jurisdiction of this court would enjoy a high input from social services and essentially, must include all disposals available in order to enable the justice to make the most appropriate decision for each offender.

## *CONCLUSION*

Since the Commission of the Peace was instituted local men and women have been appointed to adjudicate in matters which concerned the area where they live and work. The vast bulk of criminal offences are petty or minor but this does not mean they are not important. Constant petty crime is destructive and demoralising for the community. Since the public pay for crime by being both the victim and the taxpayer they rightly feel that their voice is important. The justice, as both a member of the public and a trained sentencer, can understand the problems of each side and deal with the offender accordingly. The rarified atmosphere of the legal world is enhanced by the involvement of lay people who can help to bridge the gap between ordinary members of the public and the professionals.

In the four hundred years since the inception of the justice of the peace crimes have changed very little and the weaknesses of human nature are as evident today as in the past. Justices deal with offences which may not be regarded as being on the same level of seriousness as armed robbery or murder, but which destroy the quality of everyday life for people living in the towns, cities and rural areas. Breach of the peace, drunkenness, vandalism and assault are common happenings in town centres and many other public places. The instinct, understanding and experience of the world outside the court is invaluable to justices in making their decisions on sentencing. The problems of 'what to do with them?' have not disappeared and balancing the seriousness of the offence with the financial situation of the accused with due regard to public opinion and common sense is still the almost impossible demand facing the justice.

It is a remarkable testament to the office of the justice of the peace that throughout its history, it appears to have been almost completely free of corruption. In America where the judges are not only elected but are political figures there is real concern about corruption or bias. Expectation of openness and accountability within public office have brought about changes and to that end the advisory committee now publishes the names of its members . Interested parties can put forward a name to the advisory committee who may interview the applicant, and all members have the right of veto. In addition to this the local justices' committee decides which justices will sit on the court rota and can remove a justice from the rota if required.

The office of justice of the peace has gone full circle and once more has a respected and valued position in the judicial system, but justices must strive to retain that place if it is to survive another 400 years. The office has evolved over the centuries to keep pace with developments outside the court and has adapted to meet those challenges. Training of justices locally, regionally and nationally has been embraced enthusiastically with help and advice freely given by judges and other professionals within the criminal justice system.

The principles of lay justice remain unaltered since the earliest years in England and as Hutcheson wrote in 1815 'it will appear that the discharge of important duties is expected from country gentlemen. Under free constitutions, the interest of the crown and its subjects can never be opposite. Private individuals, therefore, without risk or jealousy, may be entrusted with the execution of public functions.' Today, for the words 'private individuals' we could substitute 'men and women', in fact, 'all manner of people.'

## References

1 White Paper on J.P.s and Justice Courts CP 5241 (1973).

2 Bankowski, Hutton and McManus, *Lay Justice* (Edinburgh 1987).

3 Thomas Skryme, *The Changing Image of the Magistracy* (1983).

4 Scottish Consumer Council, *Court Reports: a Review of Facilities in Scotland's District Courts* (1990).

5 *Criminal Justice (Scotland) Act 1980*

6 *Criminal Procedure (Scotland) Act 1995*

7 For the Perth and Kinross experiment see Scottish Consumer Council, *Can Anyone Get on These?* (1990) and I Innes, *Finding and Training the Right People* (1990).,

8 Scottish Office, *Costs, Sentencing Profiles and the Scottish Criminal Justice System 1996.*

9 Bankowski, Hutton and McManus, *op. cit*, p183.

# *Bibliography*

Ascoli, David *The Queen's Peace* Hamish Hamilton (1979)
Atkinson, Mabel *Local Government in Scotland* (Edinburgh 1904)
Bankowski Z, Hutton N, McManus J. *Lay Justice* Clark (Edinburgh 1987)
Black, N. G *The Law Relating to Scottish County Councils* (1829)
Boyd, Robert *The Office, Powers, and Jurisdiction of His Majesty's Justices of the Peace and Commissioners of Supply* 2 Vols. (Edinburgh 1787)
Burney, E. *JP Magistrate, Court and Community* Hutchinson (London 1979)
Cameron, J *Prisons and Punishment in Scotland* Canongate (1983)
Carmichael, Elizabeth K *The Scottish Commission of the Peace 1707-1775* (PhD thesis) University of Glasgow (Glasgow 1977)
Defoe, Daniel *A Journal of the Plague* Year (1722)
Dow, F D *Cromwellian Scotland* John Donald (Edinburgh 1979)
Dunbar, John Telfer, *The Costume of Scotland* (London 1984).
Ferguson, W *Scotland 1689-Present Day* Oliver and Boyd (Edinburgh 1968)
Glassey, Lionel J.K. *The English JP. 1675-1720* (PhD thesis) Oxford University (Oxford 1972)
Baron David Hume *Commentaries on Crime* (Edinburgh 1797).
Hutcheson, Gilbert *Treatise on the Offices of Justice of the Peace; Constables; Commissioners of Supply with occasional Observations upon other Municipal Jurisdictions* 4 Vols (Edinburgh 1806).
Irons, J.C *Scottish Justices Manual* 2nd edition, Green (Edinburgh 1937).
Lynch, Michael *Scotland: A New History* Century (London 1991).
Malcolm, C. A ed. *Minutes of the J.P.s for Lanarkshire 1707-23* (1937).
Milton, Frank. *The English Magistracy* (Oxford 1967)
Mitchison, Rosalind *Lordship to Patronage* E.U.P (Edinburgh 1983).
Mitchison, Rosalind A *History of Scotland* Methuen (London 1970).
Moir, E *The Justice of the Peace* Penguin (London 1969).
Pagan, C D *Justice of the Peace Handbook* Wm Hodge (Edinburgh 1955).
Pryde, George S *Scotland: 1603-Present Day* Nelson (Edinburgh 1962).
Scottish Office *Handbook For Newly Appointed Justices* (Edinburgh 1998).
Scottish Record Society *The Court Book of Shetland 1602-1604* (1954).
Skyrme, Sir T, *History of the Justices of the Peace* Rose (Chichester 1991).
Skyrme, SirT, *The Changing Image of the Magistracy* MacMillan (1983).
Smith, J Irvine, in *An Introduction to Legal History* Stair Society (1958).

Smout, T C ed. *Scotland and Europe 1200-1850* Donald (Edinburgh 1962).
Thomson, J *Practical Handbook for Justices of the Peace in Scotland* Wm. Hodge (Edinburgh 1920).
Walker, David *A Legal History of Scotland.* Vol 1 Green (Edinburgh 1988).
Walker, J *Justice of the Peace Manual* Wm. Hodge (Edinburgh 1931).
Walker, Nigel *Sentencing in a Rational Society* Penguin (1969).
Whetstone, A *Scottish County Government in 18th & 19th Centuries.* John Donald (Edinburgh 1981).

Acts of the Parliament of Scotland (APS).
Calendar of State Papers (CSP).
Register of the Privy Council (RPC).
Historical Manuscripts Commission (HMC).
Royal Commission Report on Justices of the Peace (1821).
Royal Commission Report on Scotch Courts (1825).
Royal Commission Report on Justices of the Peace CP 5250 (1910).
Royal Commission Report on Justices of the Peace CP 7463 (1948).
White Paper on J.P.s and Justice Courts CP 5241 (1973).

Sederunt Book of the Justices of the Peace of the County of Dumfries 1763-99 (Ewart Library, Dumfries)
Sederunt Book of the Justices of the Peace of the County of Nairn
Sederunt Book of the Justices of the Peace of the County of Kirkcudbright
Sederunt Book of the Justices of the Peace of the County of Peebles
(all held in West Register House, Edinburgh)

## *Some Other Saltire Publications*



## *About the Saltire Society*

The Saltire Society was founded in 1936 at a time when many of the distinctive features of Scotland's culture seemed in jeopardy. Over the years its members, who have included many of Scotland's most distinguished scholars and creative artists, have fought to preserve and present our cultural heritage so that Scotland might once again be a creative force in European civilisation. As well as publishing books the Society makes a number of national awards for excellence in fields as diverse as housing design, historical publication and scientific research. The Society has no political affiliation and welcomes as members all who share its aims. Further information from The Administrator, The Saltire Society, 9 Fountain Close, 22 High Street, Edinburgh. EH1 1TF Telephone 0131 556 1836.